ability to relate, connect, and impact relationships positively, this will do it in abundance."

Paul B. Carroll, veteran journalist and bestselling author; editor-in-chief at Insurance Thought Leadership

"While most books are written about a single topic, *Shift Your Thinking for Success* contains a diversity of brief points, many of which have the potency of a whole book. Dean's ability to synthesize principles into actionable steps has made a remarkable difference in my professional life. He gets it, perhaps because he's lived it. In my opinion, Dean is one of the great communicators of modern times, and I'm sure you'll agree."

Lauren Ellermeyer, president, Beyond Fifteen Communications

"Although an endorsement from the wife of the author may seem a bit biased, I can honestly tell you after proofing the first draft of the book that my confidence level was raised dramatically. I began to see things differently and I made some radical life decisions that I probably would not have made had I not read *Shift Your Thinking for Success*. It was life-changing for me, and although I'm married to this wonderful man, I will reference this book often and will recommend it to everyone I meet."

Kitt Del Sesto, happy wife of Dean Del Sesto

"Dean has artfully crafted a wise, generous, and graceful portrait of the critical ways we can choose to show up in life to make a significant difference. Profound and valuable 'Ahas!' await his readers and will propel them, and others, forward. I'm excited to share this with many leaders."

Todd Kemp, principal and leadership coach, NorthWise Group

"*Shift Your Thinking for Success* is another one of Dean's poignant and original transformational works! With the power of a freight train, it assaults every attitude, behavior, and belief that doesn't work in our business lives and provides alternative thinking that will radically transform your life. Page by page, it encourages us to be better, so we can find greater success and fulfillment at work and in life."

Daniel L. Tocchini, founder, D3 Digital; author of *US* and *In the Twinkle of an "I"*

"Unlike books that focus on a single, in-depth topic, *Shift Your Thinking for Success* covers just about every area of business and does so in a way that is

profound. Beyond that, it has a way of clarifying, inspiring, and moving one to act that few books do."

Dave Dias, vice president, InterWest; author of *Sales Ethos: Building Long Term Client Value*

"Dean is a clear thinker who knows how to make the reader of his books the hero of his message. As you read *Shift Your Thinking for Success*, you will discover brilliance that is concise and extremely relevant for business today. You will read it and learn how to position yourself in all areas of business."

Sanford Coggins, CEO, VisionWise Capital

"A refreshing twist on the traditional approach to success. Dean has a keen ability to flip thinking that doesn't work with clear and sustainable concepts. To focus on the value of who you are, along with the awareness of the performance of your personal brand and its impact on others as the sustainable measure of success, is simply brilliant. This shift in thinking is long overdue. It is timely, relevant, and will elevate the accomplishments of any professional or entrepreneur. I'm confident this book will change lives and develop better leaders. Set your next goal to take in the ideas in this book and let this shift radically redirect your vision of success."

Gary Sikes, president/CEO, Elevation

"It's refreshing to discover a book that allows you to read quick bits of transformational information that cover a diversity of business and organizational topics. Although the items are quick reads, the potency of each point will bring business professionals as well as entrepreneurs to healthier, more productive outcomes in all of business."

Rod Baker, president/CEO, Rod Alan; co-author of *Extraordinarily You*

"This book is a road map and manual for any person looking for the practical tools to pivot their life and career. Dean masterfully explores the internal conversations that frame our engagement with others, and then shows how you can shift both the internal conversations and the resulting changes in your external context in a meaningful and planned way. Dean's matter-of-fact style of addressing key issues helps you shift both your mindset and skill set in ways that will set you up for success in your next big pivot."

Hendre Coetzee, CEO, Center for Advanced
Coaching; international trainer and speaker

"While many management books are about tactics and techniques, *Shift Your Thinking for Success* is more about who you are and less about what you do. Dean's clever and creative wit will help you discover viewpoints, mental shifts, and strategic behaviors that will help you build relationships that will lead you toward greater success in both life and work. Dean is spot-on! You are your own brand, so make it a great and memorable one. Who doesn't want to be more successful in work and life? Dean has the answers . . . seventy-seven to be exact."

Milan Yerkovich, founder, Relationship 180; marriage counselor;
co-author of *How We Love* and *How We Love Our Kids*; cohost of
the nationally syndicated counseling talk show *New Life Live*

"Dean's book *Shift Your Thinking for Success* is a powerful book for all professionals. His work is so eloquently written, and I highly recommend this book for your personal development library."

Lisa Caprelli, radio host and bestselling author of *Color Your
Message: The Art of Digital Marketing & Social Media*

"Dean Del Sesto cares about people: how they show up, how they think, how they are perceived, how they succeed. I know because he's helped me and my family in numerous ways. This book will cause you to think about the you who shows up to the world, and it will challenge you to be a better person—the one you really want to be. I know you'll grow as you read *Shift Your Thinking for Success*."

Greg Leith, CEO, Convene CEO Forum

"As you strive to become more accomplished in business, the book you hold in your hands will become a true North of sorts. This book isn't a how-to, it is a book of truths that reminds you of who you really are, what you have to offer, and how you plan to maximize life and business. *Shift Your Thinking for Success* brings self-awareness and confidence that will put you in the top 1 percent of successful people in business if you apply what you read."

Noah Elias, entrepreneur; author of *#Fearhunters*

"In the modern marketplace our reputation can rise and fall—with life-altering results. Years of steady effort can be thwarted by a succession of miscues that turn momentum from the path of success to the dustbin of defeat. If managing our own brand is mission-critical for business professionals, it's equally crucial for any serious contender who understands the underlying importance of their own personal stature in the unforgiving world of public image and earned reputation. Within these pages, Dean Del Sesto packs in consulting worth thousands that could help you experience success that's priceless. Follow his counsel and win!"

Bob Shank, CEO, The Master's Program and
Priority Living; author of *Life Mastery*

"*Shift Your Thinking for Success* over-delivers for anyone wanting to better themselves in business. From the moment you start reading, this book shows you how to think more confidently and boldly about every aspect of your business life and does so in a way that is simple and easy to read, yet hits hard in every area of business. Whoever reads this will be a different person at the end of doing so."

Beth Ganem, CEO, Organizational Development, The Ganem Group

"Want immediate improvement in your work and life? Dean cuts through the self-help noise and offers you a gift that hits home instantly. Then his ideas get better with age. Highly recommended."

Dane Sanders, founder, Fastermind.co; author, *Fast Track Photographer* and *The Fast Track Photographer Business Plan*

"You'll quickly realize in reading *Shift Your Thinking for Success* that Dean is a different, disruptive thinker who looks at everything through the lens of 'realistic change.' If you *don't* want to grow and move to new levels in your life, this book is not for you. By its nature it is designed to drive the reader to reach their full potential in life and in business, and it will do so in a simple, pragmatic, and laser-like manner."

Rick McCarthy, CEO coach; author of the book series *Defining Moments: Hearing from God During Faith-Based Travels*

"A wise friend, Alan Kay, inventor of the personal computer, once said that 'context is worth 80 intelligence quotient points.' Now, another wise friend, Dean Del Sesto, has written a breakthrough book providing context that should boost our emotional quotient at least that much. Business is about relationships, and if you're looking for a read that will help improve your

SHIFT
YOUR
THINKING
FOR SUCCESS

SHIFT YOUR THINKING

FOR SUCCESS

77 Ways to Win at Work
and in Life

DEAN DEL SESTO

Revell

a division of Baker Publishing Group
Grand Rapids, Michigan

© 2018 by Dean Del Sesto

Published by Revell
a division of Baker Publishing Group
PO Box 6287, Grand Rapids, MI 49516-6287
www.revellbooks.com

Special edition ISBN 978-0-8007-3609-5
ISBN 978-0-8007-2898-4

Printed in the United States of America

Library of Congress Cataloging-in-Publication Control Number:
2018007142

18 19 20 21 22 23 24   7 6 5 4 3 2 1

In keeping with biblical principles of
creation stewardship, Baker Publishing Group advocates the responsible
use of our natural resources. As a
member of the Green Press Initiative, our company uses recycled
paper when possible. The text paper
of this book is composed in part of
post-consumer waste.

Introduction

At work and in life, we are a brand to everyone we know or meet, which always impacts our success favorably or negatively. The question we should ask ourselves from time to time is, As a brand today, would I buy myself or keep on shopping?

It's safe to say we'd all like to be more successful, but success isn't just determined simply by what happens in our lives but also by how we think about what happens, relate to what happens, and how we govern over our mind. Meaning, our mindset is both the pathway and the barrier to our professional performance and experiencing true success. So if you're looking to elevate performance and progress in your personal and professional life, one way to succeed is to strengthen the values, qualities, and habits that comprise the brand of *you*. The fastest, most productive, and most rewarding way to improve the brand you are is to bring more focused, refined, and strategic ways of thinking to drive new attitudes, beliefs, and behaviors.

Oddly enough, though, when I ask others how much time they spend refining their thought life, the responses are usually some form of "Well, I haven't given it much thought" or "It's never really crossed my mind" or "I'd have to really think about that." Despite little consideration, the mind is the epicenter that frames and drives success and ultimately determines our progress. The effects of how we preside over our thinking in every aspect of our day will either have us accelerating backward, remaining stuck and unable to move from an unfulfilling reality, or gaining momentum with relative ease and having a great time doing it. Our thought life is our biggest opportunity or our biggest liability, if you take a moment and just . . . well . . . *think* about it.

> True success is being fully content with where you are now, while you are in the process of becoming the best that you can be.

The good news is it doesn't take massive changes in thinking to align more clearly with success. Even subtle, consistent shifts in the way we think about ourselves, our career potential, and our relationships will immediately strengthen the person we are and how others perceive us, and will give us confidence to do extraordinary things we may not have thought possible. There are ways of thinking about every aspect of our professional life with a mindset that will hold the impossible as doable, problems as opportunities, stress as a motivator, and success as achieved, positioning us to be on top at work rather than work always climbing on top of us. We can become a master of any relationship, circumstance, or vision if (and only if) we are able to shift our thinking on the fly to contend with all the difficult and wonderful realities of living a high-performance professional life.

To set expectations from the onset, *Shift Your Thinking for Success* is not a how-to book. How-to books tell you what to do, and although I'll be providing guidance on the most important aspects of success, a how-to approach would have you mimicking what I or others might do. I find this to be an unpredictable path with uncertain results, and candidly, mimicking me is a dangerous thing—depending on the day one would choose. This book will provide perspectives to empower you to live more successfully today while strengthening the brand that you are to be more relevant, compelling, and influential at work and in all of life.

We all know that achieving goals in our careers will get us to a better place, but it doesn't keep us there. So achieving goals can never be defined as success, only as reaching a milestone. Many people achieve astonishing goals in their lives only to find themselves discontent and questioning life and its meaning. Sometimes achieving goals can be a hindrance to maintaining true success, especially if those goals are defined by society's misguided view of success (the house, the boat, the car, the travel, the "whatever").

When I ask a roomful of professionals to define success, I always receive different spins but a similar theme: "When I get to a certain place, acquire certain things, or reach a certain position or status, I will be successful. Until then, I will not see myself as successful." Seeing success in this light is a guaranteed way to remain discontent and is also an impediment to making progress and reaching the goals we say are important to us. Not only that, but our confidence is greatly diminished when we showcase ourselves in an "un-arrived, just not there yet, not successful" state of being. This deception about success is the reason a high percentage of professionals today remain unsatisfied at work and why a high percentage of the population remain unsatisfied in life.

> True success is never a goal away; true success is always a belief away.

A successful career or personal life will never be found in the goals we achieve or the material things we acquire, as those things can be gone in a moment. Success can only be defined by who we *are* while doing the things we are doing. It is revealed in our character and competence. The simplest way to put it is that success is found in our perspectives, engagement, and execution in *all* things while on the path of achieving in our careers. In other words, it's not what excellence gets us that is important; it's what it builds into us that counts. It creates a mindset so durable, so stable, and so free of limitations that it installs success immediately into your presence and creates confidence internally where it matters.

The healthiest way of looking at success is that it comes from the inside out and not the outside in. Success is never determined by anything that exists in the world, but instead by what will spill out into our world from inside of us when we move through life with a brilliant mindset, a healthy attitude, and relational acuity. Don't get me wrong: success can always be enhanced by external or material things, but it is never defined or kept alive by them, as they are temporary at best—especially in today's unpredictable world.

In this book, you will learn to shift from the traditional understanding of success ("What I achieve and what I acquire") to something more meaningful, rewarding, and potent ("Success is found in who I am, who I am becoming, and the brand that is resonating with others"). In the awareness of our brand's performance and its effect on others, success comes to life, opportunities multiply, and our emotions become grounded in who we are, not just in what we have. This brings resilience, certainty, and an abundance of new resources to work with.

> Acknowledging that our brand at work can improve with a simple decision will replace circumstantial confidence with settled confidence, immovable by anyone or any situation.

As you dig into *Shift Your Thinking for Success* day to day or week to week, know that the goal is not to read to get to the next point. There is no planned correlation between the points other than they all work together to help build the amazing brand of *you*. The goal is to read and incorporate the points into your life at a pace that brings transformation, not just realization; to shift attitudes and behaviors to generate substantive breakthroughs in every area of your life. Each page will provide legitimate and meaningful ways to more efficiently reach the goals you have and will make that process a more gratifying experience while eliminating many of the ups and downs associated with work and life. This book will confirm that lasting success can only be found in the way we live life, and not through bondage to what we attain or don't attain in life.

Here's a rarely talked about fact: Those who focus on the *way they go about* their business rather than *what they are getting* in business somehow receive more from business . . . and life. Much more.

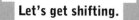
Let's get shifting.

1. A strong personal brand wears in over time, never out.

Whether you're on the ground floor or the C-level, your personal brand image is in a constant state of development, being built in the things you think, do, and say. Your impact on others never stops, and it's built in the seconds and minutes of your performance. Every choice, every action, and the attitudes that go with them count for those serious about building success and having a great brand. Taking ownership of this principle will drive awareness that every conversation, project, sale, interaction, and initiative is an opportunity to add brand equity or take it away. What you are committed to and how well or poorly you execute your tasks and your role makes the difference between your brand being an asset or a liability to your life. But what exactly is our personal brand and why does it matter?

Brand is one of the more obscure business terms. I'm in the branding business, and it took me years of learning to get the full scope of its meaning. Some see it as a promise, others as an image. Some see it as an experience, and others as an attribute. No matter what answer is given to define a brand, *every answer is correct*. Brand is defined by how every aspect of it affects people . . . *individually*, down to every detail. As such, the definition of a brand that brings opportunity for growth in your career is this: your brand is the "total combined experience" those you work with have with you in every area of the relationship. It includes how you dress, communicate, listen, and prepare for meetings; the thoroughness of your work; how you handle conflict; the value you deliver; your attitude; and so on.

I've listed just a few brand attributes out of hundreds. For example, let's talk about eye contact. Imagine three scenarios of talking with someone. In one there is an awkward or prolonged absence of eye contact; the second has just the right amount of eye contact; in the third you experience the stalker-like, strange, way-too-much, "get out of my face" eye contact. Three brands of eye contact, all affecting the image conveyed. Bottom line? Improving our brand involves the big things down to the details and everything in between.

> Your personal brand is "on" 24/7—always communicating, resonating, and impacting your life.

You can trust that those around you are constantly evaluating how you are performing and contributing to the company or to their life personally. *Evaluation, measurement, judgment* . . . whatever the term, we are always under scrutiny at some level from everyone in our realm of influence. Human beings never stop discerning. It's a survival mechanism that is very valuable in determining who we can trust, who we like, who to choose to get the job done, who we should invite, introduce, promote, and more. The people you know well— even those who know you casually—are continually forming opinions, establishing feelings, and setting up criteria to assess and clarify the brand of *you* whether you like it or not. No one can run from that.

So back to the question: As a brand, would you buy yourself or keep shopping? This question should be considered in both your career and personal life. We are a brand not only as a professional but also as a mother, father, son, daughter, spouse, friend, partner—or even casual acquaintance. Our brand is always acting as an asset to others or a liability, building brand equity or creating deficits.

I must admit, there are many times in my life as a CEO and professional when I've asked myself that question. By being honest and taking an inventory of my performance at the time, frankly, I would not have bought myself, nor bought into my vision or trusted my words. In fact, as a service to mankind, I would have done the only honorable thing: I would have told everyone to keep shopping for a better option. The good news is, in every area of our lives our brand is always upgradable.

 Look at the various categories of your life and take inventory of the brand you are today.

2. Keeping your personal brand intact is like treading water: once your effort stops, things go down from there.

Our brand is influenced by relationships, and every relationship is like a bank account. In some relationships you have a healthy balance, in others you may be nearing bankruptcy. Your relationship with every colleague, vendor, associate, employee—even friend or family member—has a relational bank account filled with equity that has multiple points of value. For example, based on the fact you're on page 15, you've only known me (through my writing) for about fifteen minutes. Based on the level of interest I've created so far, I have amassed a certain level of equity in my brand bank account with you. I may have a small amount of equity. Or perhaps the account is looking pretty healthy, and you're looking forward to reading more. Maybe I'm just about bankrupt; you may stop reading and look for the receipt. So in fifteen minutes or so, you've formed a very concrete opinion of me, and you'll continue to on every page. You probably even assessed part of my value when you first saw the cover of my book. There's no way I can get around that.

A few years ago, one of my larger business development clients called, concerned because one of their key clients was considering canceling their annual contract worth millions of dollars and several jobs. They didn't know the scope of the problem, but their relational account (their brand as perceived by the customer) had gone from years of solid health and profitability to a level that was anemic at best. My recommendation was for the client to engage in some deep due diligence with not only that client but others as well, as I believe breakdowns usually show up elsewhere. The discovery process revealed that delivery times were inconsistent and account reps were making promises that were not being kept by the service team. As suspected, similar breakdowns had occurred with other customers. At the same time, their closest competitor was providing my client's customer with solid proof that they would deliver on time—providing references to that end. The competitor's brand account was building equity before there was even a formal relationship, while my client's account was shrinking to the point of closure. According to several clients, there wasn't one big thing that was straining the relationships, but instead a buildup of consistently broken commitments and small annoyances that were fragmenting the brand of the people in the company: trust to get the job done was eroding quickly. The client made a series of new commitments and improved some strained relationships, but unfortunately wasn't able to save their biggest client relationship. As I said, our brand is what it is, and the outcomes of our performance are dependent on results—sometimes with grace, *most times not.*

> The brand you are has equity. It is a very real and tangible currency that can be spent or invested in any number of relationships, initiatives, or goals when it is needed.

Since every relationship in your life has a current account balance, making *consistent* deposits of value into the account will be essential to keeping equity in every relationship so it can withstand small, or even large, withdrawals here and there. Relational accounts left near overdrawn are always in jeopardy of closure, and relationships not sown into are usually a few small breakdowns or one large event away from insolvency. But remember, it's typically not one big event that trashes a relationship. People understand an occasional mistake, small or big. It's generally a series of consistent small breakdowns that compromise the fabric of the relationship and what is possible with it.

Make some deposits into your relational accounts today.

3. Self-evaluation is much like self-surgery. There are better, more precise options available.

Not sure about you, but I have discovered on more than a couple thousand occasions as a CEO and professional that the opinion I had of myself was a little or a lot higher than the opinions of those I worked with had of me. I've discovered that part of my human condition included an ongoing need to invent and protect my own view of my image—more specifically, to keep myself from the truth of what was real about my performance so I could maintain the image I thought I needed to succeed. Early on in my career, I rarely if ever checked in with those around me to see how I was *actually* performing. Instead, I adjusted my own view of myself based *not* on what was true and apparent to clients and other professionals, but based on what I felt I needed my view of myself to be at that time.

Soon after my epiphany on self-evaluation, I decided to request a comprehensive evaluation from my entire company on how I was performing as a business leader. I was hoping to get some thoughts on how I could improve, so I put a disclaimer in the email that I was looking for unvarnished, brutally honest feedback. It was risky, but I knew anything other than the authentic truth was going to be useless. I suggested that the evaluations be turned in via hard copy and anonymous in the same font and font size.

I had about seventy-five employees at the time, and before reading any detailed feedback from the surveys, I noticed that only seventy-four were turned in. The deadline had passed, A few days later, one of my executives walked into my office, shut the door behind him, and sat down in front of my desk. He had a look of intensity on his face, and something told me this was going to get uncomfortable in a hurry—not for him, but for me. He said, "Dean, I didn't turn in my evaluation because honestly you really are not participating in this agency with any sense of commitment. You're present, but you're not in the game and your brand within the agency is at a low right now. You come into meetings with half-hearted participation because you are very good at what you do, but people don't think you are in the trenches with them and we need you to be fully engaged."

Some CEOs may have taken offense. Instead, in a moment of humility, I said, "Thank you for caring enough about me to be honest. Tell me more."

It took a great deal of courage for him to come in and share the fullness of his and other employees' experience with me. I could've read all the evaluations in the world, and nothing would've been more impactful than what took place in a face-to-face meeting where the truth was told, heard, and felt at full impact. Although it was one of the more abrupt and abrasive rounds of feedback, it was a transformational time that spurred life-changing decisions for me. Without my colleague sharing the truth and me encouraging him to tell me more, I wouldn't have chosen the path I chose. We still work together to this day. I consider him one of my most valuable friends and business partners and the *brand he is to me* is truth, care, courage, boldness.

> A relationship stretched to new levels of transparency
> will never return to its original façade.

The first step to improving the brilliant brand of you is to discover the brand you are *today*. The best way to go about doing that is to create an environment for those around you to be truthful about how you are showing up in their life—at work, at meetings, and more. But there's a challenge—more like a disease—that gets in the way of obtaining this life-changing feedback. Some call it the practice of political correctness; I call it the art of self-protection. People are so careful to never say the wrong thing, ruffle any feathers, or make anyone dislike them, that they'd rather say nothing at all than share their truth. This is why years go by without someone telling you things that should have been shared long ago, and it's a major reason we can stay in breakdowns without knowing what our breakdowns are—breakdowns being anything that creates problems in our life or keeps us from our full potential. It's imperative to seek out this feedback. Hunt for it rather than wait for it, because it will most likely not come on its own.

Here are simple methods for getting feedback.

- List some names of people you respect—those who you work with on a regular basis. There's no rule for who or where the best feedback can come from. Sometimes the most unlikely sources can provide valuable insights that can forever change your life, the trajectory of your career, and the success you have.
- Take initiative in getting feedback from each person. The way I approach this these days is to either email or walk up to someone in the office and say, "Hey, can we get a cup of coffee or have lunch sometime? I'd like to get some feedback on some things that I think you might be able to help me out with—my treat." The added value here is that it honors people when you ask for their opinion, and you'll rarely, if ever, get a no answer. If they do say no, they may not be the kind of person you'd want to receive feedback from anyway.
- Sit down and have a real conversation. When I sit down with a person, I generally get specific about my desire to get raw, uncut feedback, and I let them know that I am not looking for the good as much as I am the bad and the ugly (the blind spots). Sometimes I'll provide the person the nature of the feedback I'm looking for in advance, so they have time to process and provide the most meaningful feedback. It's also wise to let them know you won't get defensive or hold anything against them and will keep the conversation completely confidential. You will be taking your relationship to a new level of trust, and it should remain at that level for the future.

> We are dynamic, not static—always growing,
> always changing—so it's good to get
> feedback on our current performance.

Here are some example comments and questions you can use to open things up:

- I've been looking for ways to improve my performance at work and wanted to see if I have any blind spots, things I'm not seeing, recommendations you might have.
- Are there things you see I am doing that I should stop doing?
- Are there things I'm not doing that I should be doing?
- Are there things that I'm doing that are working well and I should continue doing? Are there more effective ways you think I can serve the company?
- Does my attitude bring inspiration or perspiration to others?
- Are there others in the company whose feedback I might benefit from?

As your conversation progresses, you can get more specific about your job responsibilities and get into some of the finer details of how you're performing. Don't be surprised if during the process, the person you're speaking with opens up and requests the gift of honest feedback from you. Be ready for that possibility. Of course, always thank them for their honesty, let them know you'll act on it, and go back and share the results with them. People love to hear the impact of their feedback.

It reveals something very positive about your character when you desire to improve and are willing to open yourself up to evaluation. Once those around you have given you feedback, they'll be able to do it again, often with more candor and value due to the trust that's been built.

Consider whose feedback might be relevant, and set up a coffee conversation or two today.

4. Don't get wrapped up in the difficulties of your career; focus on how you can effectively relate to and *overcome* them.

The fact that what you "think" about an event or outcome can manifest in your mind as equal or greater than the actual event or outcome itself should get us curious. Is this make-or-break tool (your mind) being used to serve you or unnerve you at work? Is it giving you more confidence walking into meetings or leaving you uncertain, even fearful? Does it have you looking at future personal growth with optimism and confidence, or wanting to blur out the future because dealing with the present is intense enough and there's not enough mental resolve in the tank to dream? Is your mind being used to support and encourage your value or grind away your confidence and worth—making the workday something to drudge through instead of something to thrive in? I've faced all of these questions at times. I still do.

Much of our life involves processing our mental inventions of what will happen or analyzing the way something went. The question becomes, How inventive, intentional, and focused are you being with the tool that drives everything you do, say, believe, feel, and experience? The answer, as mentioned earlier, is often, "Well, I haven't given it that much thought."

The truth is, we are always in thought; thus, you cannot *not* think. But there's a difference between thinking and framing. Thinking is an automated physiological process; framing thoughts, bringing context to and controlling them, is a choice we make. Framing our thoughts is simply the process of spending enough time with them to shape them exactly the way that we want them to be. The problem is that we often move so quickly through life that we rarely slow down to rethink and reframe anything.

> In today's frenetic world, slow is the new fast, calm is the new strength, and perspective is the new profitability.

What is the trajectory of your thought life? How are you framing thoughts? How intentional are you about governing your mind? These are all questions that need to be answered to live and work successfully. If your mind is running without any real governance, your mind will have its way with you rather than you being at the helm of command central—taking control and claiming rights to what you think and how it affects your life. A healthy, maturing thought life is comprised of minute-by-minute decisions to take thoughts captive, work with them, mold them, and even beat them into submission if needed so they don't build up and dominate your mindset. It's that, or the mind runs wild, and we all know what that looks and feels like. It's not pretty. Speaking of not pretty . . .

Just prior to signing my contract to write this book, my wife and I decided to get away from work and take a little rest. We had just gone through moving our home, my father passed away rather suddenly, and I wanted to spend some time away working on the book. We decided to switch out our time-share in Carmel, California, and spend some time in the wine country, a first for us. Having never had a bad time-share experience, we were looking forward to our trip.

While driving the final few miles, the navigation blurted out, as she always does, "You are approaching your destination; your destination is on the left." We were in a pretty run-down area, and I thought, "Oh, she's got to have this wrong, please be wrong." But the next words she blurted out were "You have arrived at your destination." "*Ohhhhhhh, take it back*," I said to my wife with a groan. I didn't want to be too pessimistic, but as we drove onto the property, I noticed the rooms, or units, were on wheels, parked closer together than pickles in a jar, and the units themselves . . . *just* a little larger than a jar of pickles. I freaked (internally, of course), as this was nothing close to what we were expecting or what the pictures showed.

> You drive the emotions of your life. No one and
> no thing has the right to take the wheel.

Upon checking in, I asked if we could see our pickle jar prior to committing, so we went to visit unit #43 (*Richard Petty's number*, I thought, *and a good sign, perhaps*). We walked in and immediately the waft of chemical fruit filled our nostrils, like those Christmas-tree air fresheners you see hanging from rearview mirrors (a thousand of them). It was so strong we felt instant nausea. Back to check-in we went. Option 2, touted as a nonsmoking room, smelled like a family of chain-smokers just checked out five minutes before we arrived—with, of course, the added smell of chemical fruit to cover it up.

Option 3 smelled mildly of disinfectant, so we thought, okay, let's give it a shot. I could go into great detail about all that was wrong with the unit, but knowing my wife (aka "Travel Chick") felt badly about the choice, we started to frame what was right about the unit. "Well, it has a bathroom," I said. "We'll spend more time adventuring," she said. "It'll make the next place we stay seem like a palace." By the time we were done with the back-and-forth of reframing, laughing, and almost crying, we had successfully rethought this claustrophobic, poorly decorated (understatement), odor-ridden sliver of a trailer into our castle for the week. It would turn out to be one of our best vacations ever. As for the little unit, it remains a fond memory, *and I'll never go back.*

> Without a new way of thinking, progress
> stands still. Without new disciplines of
> thought, transformation cannot occur.

The process of rethinking "what is" until it becomes "what you want it to be" is a discipline worth experimenting with and refining until it becomes a repeatable best practice. It's a habit that becomes easier with each shift of thought. Because of the difficulties of career life and the competition in growth, the process of slowing down and investing time rethinking situations is invaluable on our journey of success.

Bringing some qualifiers/filters to the process will generally draw out enough thought to frame the right perspective.

- If this situation were a provision to help me grow, what would it be suited to help me grow into or out of?
- What will it take and who do I need to be in this situation to have victory over it, rather than allowing it to have its way with me?
- Who can I gain perspective from that will help me see what's possible rather than what's wrong?
- Once through this, how can I make sure I don't go through it again?

Going through these questions is a powerful thought exercise in your career, and learning them will be like learning to swim. Once you dive into the pool, somehow you get to the other side, and each time you do, it gets better, faster, and easier. At least that's what I've framed it up to be.

 Take 10. Rethink something that's set up to lose and frame it into a win today.

5. Personal mission, vision, and values drive everything you do and all that you are.

Nearly every organization on the planet starts life with mission, vision, and core values (MVV). They are the foundation of what a company stands for, where it is headed, and the way it will go about doing what it does. The challenge is that often these documents get lost in the shuffle, are poorly written, and never get driven into action or measurable results. I call this MVVDOA. For every human being in business or not, MVV should be held as foundational to their own brand, and because they are not created by committee, they can be personally crafted. The principles can be owned and activated with immediate life-changing results—if created properly.

Working closely with business professionals and CEO groups across the nation, I often am given the charge of helping them craft clear, concise, and to-the-point "personal mission, vision, and core values statements." Only about 5 percent of the people I work with actually have a document that references back to what they personally stand for, where they're headed, the character they say they are committed to, and the ways they want to conduct themselves at work. Most inherently know what they aspire to, but based on feedback I've received, when they bring a clear voice to their mission, their vision, and their ways of doing business, they'll admit it's one of the more valuable exercises they've ever done.

So where to start? There is often a great deal of confusion about the mission and vision, and how they work together with the core values, so here's a bit on their true makeup to keep this simple.

> The MVV are more than just a "you" road
> map. They're the driving force to help you be
> fully confident at being exceptionally you.

To demystify a bit, the **mission** has to do with what you stand for. It touches briefly, if at all, on what you do for a living, but focuses largely on the philosophical stance of what you desire to cause in life, business, and relationships. Most accurately, it alludes to where you most consistently make a difference in the lives of the people who are connected to your brand. Generally, it is more emotional than cerebral and more lifeline than bottom line. And yet, it will have a profound effect on everyone's bottom line if exercised to its potential.

> Your mission well executed in business will bring
> notable financial reward, but it's generally something
> you love doing so much, you'd gladly do it for free.

The **vision** focuses on what you will accomplish (and by when, if timing is a consideration). It is designed to create accountability to specific progress in the short and long term. In contrast to mission statements and core values, which remain mostly constant, the vision statement evolves over time as you live it out. Achieving the current vision is a call to adopt a new one, as are changing market conditions, economic factors, job shifts, new life initiatives, and many other personal and passion-focused variables.

Core values are the character traits you will demonstrate to accomplish the mission and the vision. They are the "ways of being" for you and your brand. They will show up in the things you do and say, as well as the nonnegotiables of what you *won't* do and say— *ever*. One's values are highly personal and are rarely changed unless one sees the need to shift into stronger values more relevant to both corporate and individual progress.

Developing MVV that resonate and move you emotionally will require a bit of "sitting under a tree" time. Whatever goes down on paper has to be inspiring enough to work itself into your mindset, heart-set, and actions *daily*.

What I see happen most in development is that a great deal of thought goes into the mission, vision, and values as they get written, but then a very common thing happens: the thoughts are crafted into the longest conceivable sentences in the history of humankind. There seems to be an odd pressure to make sure every principle in existence is included in the MVV somewhere. Then a fear sets in that if you leave something out, it just won't work. The outcome is an overly homogenized MVV that will leave us uninspired, unable to remember it, and searching for aspirin. Not a good start. If you can't retain your MVV, they are useless.

> Creating your own mission, vision, and values
> that inspire is a heart-form and an art form.

At first, write your MVV freely. Once you have a thought-deck together and you start refining, *think brevity*. It will take a bit of effort to condense what you have written into clear, concise statements, but the following example of my MVV should make the process easier. And if you happen to think mine works for you or is somewhat close, feel free to use or retrofit it in any way you see fit.

Ultimately, whatever you write should be written to grip you *emotionally* more than *logically*, as you'll be moved more by feelings than by reason. For example, my personal mission statement is ***"To be a graceful interruption to the things that don't work in people's personal and business lives."*** For me, it's short, memorable, and a good reason for me to wake up in the morning. It's a statement that reminds and empowers me to help people stop doing the things that are not working and help set the trajectory toward things that will. You'll notice a lot of that in this book, and it carries through my career and advisory work. Although there are hundreds of other things in life I don't do well, this is one that I do like a laser, and it's proven to be a valuable asset based on feedback from both individuals and companies. Although I get paid well for being an interruption to what doesn't work, it's also something that gives me the greatest joy in life—so much so, that I would do it for free (and honestly, I do it for free a lot . . . *and love it*). So when you think about creating your mission, make sure it's life-giving and not life-taking, because if it's life-taking, it's not a mission, it's more like a task or a responsibility.

My vision in life is, **"Whatever it takes, whoever I need to be, I will bring the full expression of my verbal, visual, and business talents to conversations, circumstances, and initiatives."** This focuses me on being the best of me regardless of cost or comfort. It also guarantees that if I do this well, success will be imminent on a grand scale, and I don't have to worry about a more defined vision, like "become a millionaire by the time I'm X." There's nothing wrong with that vision, it's just not my brand.

As for my core values, again I keep them simple:

1. **Think relationship before agenda.**
2. **Maintain an attitude that inspires.**
3. **Never fall asleep at the wheel of my relationships.**
4. **Lead by example, measure my results.**
5. **Above and beyond is standard practice.**
6. **Keep my word, keep it real, keep it fun.**

Again, there's little about my profession in all of these statements, and that's intentional. I want these mission, vision, and values statements to be universal so they can manifest in every area of my life at any time with no limitations. I don't want them to be dependent on location, vocation, or situation; I want them to reflect someone I am, not just something I do.

> If you can't remember your personal MVV, it's like forgetting an anniversary (not advised).

Once you have clear, memorable, and emotionally compelling MVV, then what? They say it takes thirty days to make a habit. I've discovered that habits made in thirty days typically last about ninety days. And habits made over a ninety-day period typically last a lifetime. So at the beginning of each day for ninety days read through your mission, vision, and core values; look at your day and invest a few minutes of thought on how they can be applied to what's in the day. At the end of the day take a few moments to reflect on how you performed. Then resume the following day, bring your adjustments, and refine the "improving you." Mission, vision, and values integration is a rhythm that helps you stay in step with what you believe in all circumstances with all people. Once in the rhythm of living out your MVV, you'll see opportunities opening up and you'll have more capacity to bring innovations to your life, rather than consistently wondering who you will be and/or how you will live your life.

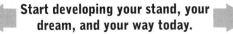

Start developing your stand, your dream, and your way today.

6. We are not just known for the job we do, but for the experiences we create and the influence that we have.

If your personal brand is your influence and influence moves people—and people are the pathway to progress and the conduit to achievement—then your personal brand is the vehicle to get you there. It's important to cement that truth early on, as we will be linking a great deal of the success principles in this book back to the brand of you that you're crafting daily.

A few years back, I was watching a brilliant celebrity newscaster give a keynote address on getting ahead in business. He kept referencing the term *juice*, his vernacular for brand reputation. He started by asking a simple question: When we call people, do we have enough juice for them to answer the phone when they see it's us? Or, a close second, will they call us back? Then he went into more detail and asked how long it takes for them to call us back. Do they call us back immediately, the following day, or six weeks later (and have to apologize for forgetting about us)? Or do we never get the call?

This is the nature of *juice*, aka our *personal brand*. We either have it with others or we don't. The value we create for people—whether in a one-time meeting or working with them on a day-to-day basis—determines how much juice we have. Juice is leverage, it is power, it is influence, and it is a deciding factor in whether you climb up the corporate ladder, stay in the same place, or get walking papers.

> Your brand is not just what you share with others, but what others share about you.

30

A while back a friend of mine was up for a promotion, and it was going to make a notable difference in her life financially. In her mind it was a lock: there was no question she would be promoted—in fact, she believed she had a "right" to be in that position. The call came with an invitation to her superior's office, and to her surprise the promotion had been given to another colleague. (Boom—out go the "rights"!)

Frankly, my friend felt her colleague didn't have nearly the experience or skills that she had, so she began to inquire about what went wrong, why she'd been passed over. She was told that in doing some departmental due diligence it was found there was a lack of relatability between her and the other team members. The company felt that leadership would be better suited in the hands of someone who had influence along with an adequate level of ability. Even though my friend had more skills and more experience, the characteristic of relatability became more important to achieve the company's objectives. I suggested that she do some homework and discover more about why she was not resonating with the team. In discovery, she found out that a dominating, know-it-all disposition was being experienced from her in different ways with those she interviewed. She was able to apologize for those behaviors and begin the process of rebuilding her brand within her department in hopes that when the next promotion came along, her brand would be intact with no obstacles in the way of her moving forward in her career.

> Listen carefully to others, and the brand you are
> will be discovered in the words that are shared.

When you consider that your brand is the "total combined experience" that others have with you, special attention needs to be given to all aspects of your image within your career. Your personal brand manifests in all kinds of juice. There's ability juice, credibility juice, personality juice, contribution juice, consistency juice, versatility juice, reliability juice, fun-factor juice, and many more. Brand influence gets incredibly granular as people evaluate you based on so many things: showing-up-on-time juice, going-beyond-what-is-expected juice, offering-to-help juice—even cleaning the coffee pot when it's empty gets you juice. Sometimes it's the small, "unexpected" things that get noticed over the *bigger* things we should already be doing.

Truth is, leaving out any aspect of your value to others is danger at work, as you'll never quite know which aspect is important at that critical time; if you're a business professional, that could mean times of promotion, reorganization, or downsizing. And for those relentless about living a life of continual fulfillment and success, influence (aka juice) is important at all times. It's the substance of your brand's makeup, and a core attribute for getting the most out of every day.

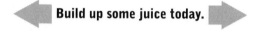 **Build up some juice today.**

7. Success will never be success if the unquenchable quest for more becomes more important than gratefulness for what you have.

There's something valuable missing from this world. In fact, I'd say about 80 percent of all people are doing life with little or none of it, 15 percent are walking around with a moderate amount, and 5 percent have a fairly healthy supply of it. That valuable thing is *gratefulness*. For some reason it eludes us with great fervor, yet it's available to us in a never-ending supply found in our choice to simply be grateful for what we have.

Although you might feel the presence of others' discontentment like a bit of irritating humidity, it's not always obvious that gratefulness is missing from people. You may have to look closely and have a conversation to experience the depth of this truth. But some provocative questions, like asking what is missing from someone's life, or what bothers them, or how they feel about work or world conditions will lead you to see that gratefulness is missing and has been replaced with discontentment. There's no shortage of negative thoughts, opinions, or attachments about what is not working for people, what they disdain, don't have, or don't like. Just pull their string and let 'em rip, and you'll have to break out a magnifying glass to find a speck of gratitude for what they have. If you want to prove the theory, in the midst of their rant conversation, just ask them what they are grateful for. By the time their emotions snap back to a baseline from the previous dump, you'll find there's unsettledness about the question. *What do you mean* grateful? *I'm not even done complaining.*

The challenge for people to consider what they are thankful for is often a shocker because it's a question rarely asked and a topic that gets lost in the chronic complaining common to our culture today. We see the lack of gratefulness in the public, the media, movies, and on TV, but if we're honest about it, the most pronounced place we see it is in our own hearts. Living in the absence of gratitude offers little in the way of upside or value to the resonance and persona of our brand.

> A universal truth is that nothing negative
> can coexist in the same space
> as gratefulness.

Whether sporadic or chronic, the subtle nature of discontentment will always benefit from an interruption. If you haven't been exposed (or even if you have), go visit a children's cancer ward, take a mission trip to a developing country, visit a prison, or simply google chronic conditions or deformities people live with and see what you find. I generally don't like to usher people into reality like this, but it is healing on a number of levels if you're willing to invest in some discomfort. It will bring a powerful realization and begin the process of reconnecting you to gratitude in many ways.

> I'm grateful for my bankruptcy. It taught me
> more about business than all of my education
> combined. I call it my "Thankruptcy."

The hard truth is that ungratefulness is a form of self-focus that just doesn't work for anyone, and to be moderately or consistently in a state of ungratefulness will weld unhappiness onto your brand and attitude regardless of what you achieve, acquire, or attain. Because gratefulness is a choice we get to make, we can bring just about anything in our life into a grateful paradigm. We can even be thankful for adversity, challenges, and problems. Consider how much you have grown through the difficulties in your life, and how without them, you would not have developed into who you are. The question is, the next time something bad happens in your life, will you be grateful when it's over or have some form of gratefulness at the onset for who you will become through the adversity?

Regardless of circumstance, Gratefulness = Great Fullness.

Appreciate the fullness of what is before you today.

8. A façade, no matter how well worn, doesn't assist you on any front.

First impressions are lasting impressions, right? True, but in business, creating a good first impression is generally more of a strategy employed to create an outcome. The challenge with first impressions is that there can be so many factors built into them that by the time the impression hits, it may look too polished, coming across as contrived, inauthentic, and in some cases manipulative or deceptive.

Today, people are reluctant to trust first impressions—so much so that they've built in processes, metrics, and emotional assessments such as Myers-Briggs to make sure the real person is seen by the time their evaluation is complete. Obviously, preparation is essential to be on your game, but impressions are foundationally made and maintained by what is true, authentic, and consistent—not what is manufactured, acted out, and immediate. Preparedness and being genuine go hand in hand, meaning the greater the preparation, the greater opportunity there is to relax and be exceptionally you while you nail it. That resonates well with people.

A few years back, I was developing the business brand for Rod Alan, a high-end custom clothing company. Their value proposition was, and still is, to customize the client's wardrobe to fit the exact nature and profile of the individual. They are detailed in their work and relentless about their process. They consider the physical attributes and personality of the client, audiences the client will be in front of, and several other key variables before procuring a fabric or designing a stitch. Rod Baker, the CEO, had a vision to make sure that every thread of clothing or accessory aligned with the authentic nature of that individual so the person would always be at ease, fully themselves with no obstruction of negative thought, feeling, or discomfort. The tagline I crafted for Rod Alan was, "Extraordinarily you." The concept worked so well with their clients that Rod and his writing partner, Rick Wagner, went on to write a book called *Extraordinarily You.* As thought leaders on personal image, they both realized the most powerful impression anyone can make begins by being extraordinarily themselves. That was the baseline for great things to happen for them, and it will always be the baseline if you trust and build on the authentic you.

> Being fully ourselves is the only foundation of self to build upon. It's that or we end up buffing our veneers and polishing our façades for a lifetime.

The ironic thing about authenticity is if we meet someone who rubs us wrong but they are totally authentic and being themselves, we somehow appreciate that they are simply being real. We respect it, are amused by it to a degree, and at times wish we could be that comfortable in our own skin. Think Clint Eastwood in *Gran Torino.* His character was toxic, bigoted, bitter, and rude. Yet he was so extraordinarily himself, he won us over immediately. And at the end of the movie when he gave the ultimate sacrifice (his life) so his neighbors could live free from the threat of the local gang, it proved that the last impression can take first place and create a legacy that will never be forgotten—regardless of what the first impression had to say.

In contrast, there are those well-mannered, well-dressed, and rehearsed people that, for some reason, we can't connect with, don't trust, or don't even like because they are being a small percentage of who they are and a big percentage of who they *think* they need to be in order to get what they want. Authenticity attracts, but façade repels. "Fake it till you make it" is a recipe for a lonely stage where the spotlight is only on you, the audience is leaving in numbers, and the bad reviews shut down the show until a new-and-improved show comes along. I know, because I speak from experience.

> They didn't feel the need to impress me. I must say, that impressed me about them.

Despite whatever the psychological circumstances of my childhood, upbringing, career, and other experiences may have to say, I must confess that I have spent thousands of hours inventing what others thought of me—so much so that I missed out on a great deal of relationships, progress, and success. As such, my presence with people was always a partial presence, and the brand impression that I left was a fragmented experience leaving the other person to invent on their own what might be going on rather than me filling in the blanks with *just being me*. But then something shifted. The following thought was a critical catalyst in one of the bigger changes in my life: *When I began to think less of what others thought of me, it was then I was really able to think*. The amount of mental bandwidth it takes to contextualize what others think of us, trying to make notable impressions, is enough bandwidth usage to reduce our capacity to think about the things that matter and better the lives of those around us. Our innovation will fall flat and our presence will be shallow because we're using so much of our mental currency on what other people think about us. Not that we should ignore constructive feedback from others as I shared earlier, but the constant imagining of what people are thinking of us is a weight we shouldn't be carrying around. And the truth is, people aren't thinking about us as much as we think they are.

There is a deserved freedom for us to be extraordinarily ourselves and be okay with that. The sooner we get down to living in that amazing space, the sooner we'll be able to be comfortable with what is true while we refine what our real brand is. It may be a bit uncomfortable at first, but the vision of investing our time in just being with others rather than impressing them will make the best possible impression we can ever make.

 Be the fully authentic you today and see what impressions come from it.

9. When integrity becomes average, it loses leverage and relationships hemorrhage.

Integrity is an interesting word. Ask just about anybody if they have integrity and more often they'll say yes—with some sort of caveat attached. And yet if you were to poll the planet and ask, "What's one thing missing in this world?" integrity and character are among the first words you'll hear. So many people proclaim they have integrity, but few people are on the receiving end of it. Hmm. It's a word that is thrown around rather loosely because the meaning of integrity is often invented on a person-by-person basis and held to standards based on past experiences, feelings, or circumstances—not a defined set of principles.

Consider that the most effective meaning of *integrity* is "the integration of our total belief system working in congruency and perpetuity." That means whatever belief system defines our character and our brand, we must achieve every aspect of it, at all times, every time, and never fail. I don't know about you, but something tells me I will be out of integrity before the week is over—or more realistically, before the day is done.

> For anyone to claim they have integrity, they have to achieve it in its real-world meaning.

So here's the rub. *Nobody owns integrity.* It's not something you can possess or even claim you have. Demonstrating integrity is an ongoing practice that knows no end, only new beginnings. The moment we think we own integrity is the moment we begin to relax in our commitment to practice it. Think about it. Why would I need to practice that which I already have or own? I'm an "integrous" person, one might say. "Integrous" by the way, is not a word (and for good reason). But the idea that we own integrity is like saying we own patience, love, or self-control.

Several years ago I was working with a vendor on a project and got a call from them just before their deadline, which was two days before my own presentation time. The programmer told me the project was not going to be completed as he had another project come up. I had to call my client and let them know that the project was not going to be done on time—not a fun experience for me. Now, I've had to delay a presentation more than once in my career for a variety of reasons. Generally, it's not a big enough hit to kill the relationship, but on one occasion, a single delay killed the account. The client shared that if this was going to be the "go forward dependability," they couldn't go down that road. It was a hard line, but I deserved it.

Back to the programmer. When I confronted my programmer on the breakdown, he got upset with me and alluded that I was questioning his integrity. And I said, "You're right, I am. You made a judgment call to put work that suited your situation in front of mine without even having the professional courtesy to call me and let me know that my job would be delayed. That would've given me plenty of time to get another programmer to fill the gap, and I could've made my presentation on time. Not only has your brand been impacted here, mine has as well." I went on to share that he was confusing integrity with selective virtue or situational integrity. I told him that I know these things happen, but he would have been able to keep the momentum of his integrity had he just called and given me plenty of time to field it to another programmer. We cleared the air and have a better working relationship because of it today.

> Integrity is the totality of your belief system in play. It is not to be confused with selective virtue or situational integrity.

Everyone has their own belief system, and it's a good idea to identify in detail what that looks like. The following twenty-five "Integrity is" statements are part of a 365/1-point-a-day poster that I produced a while back. This was the vehicle I used to begin to craft my own value system and the things I aspire to. Do I practice all of them? Of course not; as I mentioned, I don't own integrity—only do my best to practice it day by day, hour by hour, minute by minute. Here's a snapshot of the poster on integrity:

1. Integrity is a daily decision—actually hourly, but more realistically minute by minute.
2. Integrity is proactive, not reactive, in nature.
3. Integrity is completing everything you said you would regardless of how much work it is.
4. Integrity is going beyond what is "needed" into the realm of absolute excellence in all that you do.
5. Integrity is waking up earlier so you can fulfill that one dream you've been putting off so long.
6. Integrity is never complaining . . . ever.
7. Integrity is being on time . . . *every time.*
8. Integrity is focusing on what's next, not what's wrong.
9. Integrity is taking full responsibility for your own actions.
10. Integrity is taking risks knowing you'll exercise the character needed to make it happen.
11. Integrity is picking up the phone when someone in need is calling.
12. Integrity is bringing attention to the extra change that a clerk may have given you.
13. Integrity is letting the other driver in.
14. Integrity is asking if anybody would like the last piece of cake without that greedy smile on your face.
15. Integrity is treating store clerks with respect.
16. Integrity is when you enter into conflict fully considering the other's point of view.
17. Integrity is when you turn down something you want to do for something you ought to do.
18. Integrity is innovating ways to create value for others.
19. Integrity is paying attention when the speaker is speaking.
20. Integrity is writing things down so you won't forget.

21. Integrity is being authentically happy when someone gets a promotion over you whether they deserve it or not.
22. Integrity is the only viable option when in dispute.
23. Integrity is drawing out the best in people.
24. Integrity is the foundation of your reputation.
25. Integrity is sharing what is real with no worry of how that might make *you feel*.

As indicated by the sheer volume of detail integrity is comprised of, integrity is not only a high bar, it's made up of detailed thinking that has an impact on every area of your work and personal life. The more you invest into it, the more it becomes part of your practice—a practice that has worth and is incomparable in our quest toward emotional, relational, and professional success.

Consider the total picture (every area) of your integrity today.

10. Physically, are you working more "optimized" or "anesthetized"?

It may seem out of place, but I want to address health on the front end of this book so you'll know how shifts in food intake can influence your mood, energy level, presence with others, and mental sharpness. In our fiercely competitive workforce, it makes good sense to be in top physical condition to sustain the energy, focus, and stamina required to excel.

It's seldom talked about, but eating for exemplary performance at work will give you the edge you need to contend more handily with the challenges of work while you create more value for yourself and others. Keep in mind, this has nothing to do with physical weight, but more the emotional/relational and financial weight we put on ourselves by poor food intake and dwindling health.

> Unhealthy foods manifest as taffy to the gears of our mind.

A few thousand years ago (an entirely different competitive environment), I'm not sure if there was much room for physical atrophy or poor diet—hence that "survival of the fittest" quote you've heard from time to time. You had to walk everywhere, work the land to live, and the only fast food around was when you accidentally inhaled a fly while running from who knows what.

Today in our fast-paced, fast-food world of minimal physical activity, it's wise to evaluate how our physical condition affects our capacity to thrive at work. There's an old saying that "the world goes to the energetic," and although not entirely true, I recently began to wonder how food intake affected our capacity to thrive. I looked at my own situation and realized that when I ate certain foods, I became immobilized by mental lethargy, had limited stamina, and worked in a semi-foggy state. The worse I ate, the worse it got, and by paying close attention to how I felt I was able to see which foods gave me energy and which drained me. I took some time to consider how much those in my life were being impacted while I droned around in a food coma at various times. My business partners, employees, and clients were all experiencing a groggy, inconsistent, moody, semi-alert, half-committed me. I was a mess. So I changed my diet, went to the gym, and am grateful I took the steps (as are others). Here's the principle in all this: if we really take to heart how our health affects our relationships, how we perform at work, and how our health impacts our wealth, we will be more cognizant of what we put into our body and how we treat it.

Another part of health governance shows up in the duration of our work life. It is estimated that those who ignore their health shave from 5–25 years off their actual life and cut short years of effective work performance. It's a little-known fact that, on average, professionals hit the peak of their effectiveness at work a little later in life. For those with health issues, it means when business IQ is nearing maximum multiplication potential, reduced energy levels, debilitating disease, or death *may* occur or be just around the corner. This is a hard subject. It's hard, because it's real.

> Are you governing your health for maximum business performance, or are you working in physical deficiency and coping with it by labeling it as normal?

Add to that the incapacitating effects of premature lethargy or illness and the burden multiplies—and not just with us and those we work with. We pull others out of their game as they must sideline their vision to care for us or make up for our dwindling health and cover the work we can't do. Tough words, yes, but to soften them would be a disservice. Lives depend on it, your brand depends on it, and holistic success depends on it. Obviously, these are extreme realities, but it's not an extreme view.

Eat well for a higher level of performance this week. See how it feels and how much more gets done.

11. A person committed to perspiration is more effective than a person moved by motivation.

If any one word in the English language can be blamed for people not growing, making progress, or starting something, it would be the word *motivation*. "I didn't feel motivated," "The motivation just isn't there," or "I tried to get motivated, but couldn't." Motivation is the go-to blame word for things not happening, and the reason why it's so common is because it is based mainly on emotions and feelings, which are in a continual state of flux. Unfortunately, how we feel can change with little provocation, vaporizing that spring in our step into nothing in about five seconds. Motivation gone. Where it went . . . who knows?

The dictionary's meaning of *motivation* tells the story: it indicates that motivation is a willingness or desire for someone to do something. There you have it, all the progress of mankind wrapped up in willingness or desire—which in and of themselves do nothing and will dwindle if not fueled by a commitment. This commitment will be effective only if it doesn't care much about feelings and won't let them obstruct the path to getting things done.

> The quest for motivation often leads to hesitation, complication, exasperation, aggravation, and resignation.

Vulnerability time. At the onset, I didn't want to write this book . . . at least, not yet! I felt it was too soon after my first book to write a book that was close in principle but focused more on our personal brand and its effect on our work life. I wondered whether I could pull it off so soon and whether I could write something transformative. I shared with my publisher that there was another book that I wanted to write and it was well under way, but they felt this would be a logical second book based on the trajectory of my first book, *Shift Your Thinking*.

While we were in the process of going back and forth, I realized my motivation level for writing this book was nowhere near the other book I'd wanted to write for a while. However, I was beginning to see the reasoning for the publisher's direction. I decided to take a week and just commit my way into writing *Shift Your Thinking for Success*. It was somewhat difficult at first, and I wasn't connecting the dots really well, but I did something I rarely do: I paid close attention to my motivation level. It remained about the same until about thirty pages into the book. At that point, I had a sudden awareness that went beyond motivation straight into a vision for a book I believed would impact lives for good. It's like the process skipped over the need for motivation and got far enough into the commitment to connect deeply to a purpose. Well beyond a feeling, it became a cause that brought hope of a good work now and more books in the future, regardless of unstable motivation levels.

What was interesting to me is when the motivation/purpose/vision came. It didn't come before I started, which is when I thought it was needed to get things moving. It happened about 12–15 percent into the process, well after things got moving. Once I was in the rhythm, that purpose manifested in a solid *lasting drive* made evident by your eyes on this page.

> We can move from a project to commitment
> *without* motivation and get far enough into what
> we desire to create sustainable drive rather
> than the unpredictability of motivation.

So when it comes to starting something new or bringing things to a new level, consider skipping over the search for motivation and decide yourself into a commitment that creates sustainable drive. You'll find the value is in the doing and not in the overthinking or navigating your way through erratic feelings trying to form them into motivation that isn't even needed to get things going in the first place.

**Skip the motivation and dive into
the commitment today.**

12. The way you share about your work should not be mechanical, but conversational, relational, and perhaps a touch more emotional.

Where we work happens to be the place we spend most of our time during the waking hours of our week. Our job is a VERY big part of our life. And yet, if you ask most people what they do for a living, the answer is surprisingly beige, devoid of conviction, uninspiring, and often leaves questions instead of a clear understanding of what we do. The value in being resolute and emotionally connected to our job description will make itself evident by how others respond as we share. They will be interested or checked out in direct proportion to the passion we have . . . *or don't.*

> We shouldn't rest on the responsibility of others to listen, but on our ability to make certain we are heard.

There are several ways to tell people what you do for a living. For example, early on in my career I was at the dentist's office and was asked what I did for a living. I told the dentist passionately what I did to help those in business and was resolute about my value. All that expensive dental work ended up being free and I racked up about $10,000 in credit, because he hired me to brand his dental practice. How we share what we do matters, and it will matter more in some instances than it does others, so it's always good to have the approach solid. The old adage that practice makes perfect doesn't apply here, as we aren't striving for perfect, canned, or rehearsed. We're striving for a conversational approach that fits who you are. This will require practice so it sounds compelling and natural. A good job explanation, aka elevator pitch, has a balance of conviction and content so it doesn't sound like hype yet doesn't put your audience to sleep.

You can use the snapshot, short view, and the quick pitch as ways to share your role with others. You'll use them for different situations, and I recommend having some added talking points if you need to share the full value of what you deliver. One of our one-liner value points was this: "One of our clients spent $50 million with us over 5 years and we made them $950 million in profitability." Another is, "We turned a client from number 23 to the number 1 position in the country." These help to bring substance and believability to the things we do. Here are some possible scenarios:

THE QUESTION: "So what do you do?"

THE SNAPSHOT: "I'm a project manager at the largest design-build concrete contractor in the country."

THE SHORT VIEW: "I'm a project manager at the largest design-build concrete contractor in the country. Basically, we specialize in building concrete parking structures and multistory buildings."

THE QUICK PITCH: "I'm a project manager for X construction. We're one of the largest concrete contractors in the country. We design and build concrete parking structures and multistory buildings. In fact, if you've been to the MGM Grand, the Honda Center, or the Disney Grand California Hotel, you've either parked in one of our structures or walked into one of our buildings."

The fourth and best way to share what you do is to bring it into the world of the person you're talking to. For example, several years ago, after I'd been in business for about twenty-five years, my father said to me, "Dean, what exactly do you do for a living?" After all this time, he didn't know. So we both laughed a bit, and I said, "Okay, remember back when you were in the insurance business?" . . . and I went on to share with my dad what I would have done for him if he hired me back in the day. It took a couple minutes of connecting the dots into his world to do what twenty-five years somehow couldn't. He laughed at the end and said, "So now I know exactly what you do." It was a special moment for both of us. Today, when someone asks me what I do, I'll sometimes say, "Well, tell me what business you're in, and I'll give you in context what I would do for you."

It's pretty brilliant, actually—a heck of a lot less mechanical and more relevant. However you decide to share, you'll want to practice, drill, and rehearse until it can come across naturally with clarity, conviction, and a bit of empathy that connects with who you're talking to.

Take a little time and perfect your pitch today.

13. Your work ethic isn't just about what you accomplish, it's about what it does to you . . . *who you become.*

The pace of business today isn't just moving fast, it's *accelerating* fast. It seems the average pace is a frenetic urgency to reach goals at light speed and keeping up—let alone getting ahead—has become the equivalent of an Olympic sport. There's simply no room for complacency in the world of work, and any tricks, manipulations, or tactics to make us appear like we're working hard and performing well when we're not are being removed daily by processes, performance measurement, technologies, and more. This makes having an enduring and exemplary work ethic a basic requirement for success and progress.

Whether you are employed by a company or self-employed, there's a reason why millions of professionals and visionaries never get ahead or complete the visions and goals they put into play. They get excited, get things moving, and bring their goal to a point, but most of the time, things get tough and come to a grinding halt. Then the default of "something different will be better" surfaces, but after a while they hit the same wall again. This scenario plays out in large numbers; only those who embrace a strong work ethic overcome it. Olympic athletes are a great example of those who succeed: they dive in to the pain of a killer work ethic for the good of something greater than that pain.

> The days of "opportunity knocks" are over. We must hunt, chase, and capture opportunity.

As for a knock . . . I wouldn't wait around for it.

In most cases of mentorship or advisory I've been invited into, if things were not improving, growing, or succeeding, it was rarely for lack of strategy or opportunity. After some basic inquiry, I would usually uncover that a person was strategically adequate with a good direction, but their work habits—their capacity to push through adversity, spit in the eye of rejection, and do the hard work needed—were absent, along with all the strength that could have been derived from stretching to a new level of work ethic. Ironically, solid work habits inherently draw out the strategy necessary to course-correct just about any work issue and will usually create more solutions, opportunities, and strategies than are needed. Work is in some ways development and innovation in disguise. I don't want to discount strategy, as it's essential to maximize work ethic, but strategy without serious work disciplines is dangerous, as it will have you bouncing from thing to thing, thinking intelligence and strategy are the answer when a consistent work ethic will work miracles.

The real value of an improved work ethic, however, isn't so much about the obvious progress it makes; it's more about what it builds into your character and your brand. It has the capacity to take your convictions and courage and lead you to a place where no matter what is in front of you, you'll hold it with minimal fear, stress, and uncertainty, and you'll be confident your work ethic will pull you through. *And it will*, if you stay the course. This is the lasting value of an excellent work ethic, once you are in the rhythm of living it out daily.

I've advised hundreds of people who have had many starts and stops in their careers, and a look at their current vision or goal has brought a sobering reality to the table. After they shared their enthusiasm and excitement about what they're going to conquer, I would be forced to say something like, "If indeed you started and stopped a half a dozen things before and never quite pushed through the discomfort of making any one of them a reality, and you didn't employ a 'get it done' work ethic and equip yourself to achieve that level of completion, what makes you think the current goal or vision is going to be any different?" Then we'd discuss new ways of engagement that would see things to completion. Whenever you have a number of starts and stops or you've stayed stuck for a period of time, you are building a subversive inconsistency into your character and your habits. This will make it difficult to achieve anything substantial. But to push through the effort, commitment, and endurance it takes to bring just *one thing* to full maturity or radical success will position you to bring the next thing to maturity or radical success as well.

> Brilliant work ethic is a rhythm that will have you dancing down the road of progress with the ease and grace of a swan.

Whenever you bring your work ethic to an unprecedented place, you will rarely, if ever, turn back to the version of the prior you, and a new, stronger you will emerge in the process. The process is comparable to how a muscle works: staying in the commitment of the workout builds strength, stamina, confidence, and lasting change, and we all know what happens when the workouts stop. The endgame of a status-quo work ethic will turn momentum into "nomentum or slowmentum" where exemplary work ethic creates "flowmentum and growmentum." Sorry—feeling a bit poetic.

Don't just value what your work ethic gets you today; see how it builds a new you.

14. If you want to get the most out of every conversation, think relationship before agenda.

If you were to measure the results of every conversation you've ever had, you'd find that some were a liability to progress and others were incomparable in worth. Either way, at the end of every conversation, you've set up the trajectory for what's next and the relationship is further defined. Conversations are incredibly powerful and should be handled with care as they can kill progress as readily as they can promote it. So why do so many conversations *not work*?

The reason is simple—conversations are often a self-focused, one-way broadcast instead of a mutually focused two-way street. Translation? Not every conversation nor every individual needs to be a means to our end. Somewhere within the words of every conversation there is an opportunity to encourage someone in their goals, help someone with their work, or discover what's real in their world. The goal is to make some **conversational deposits** before you make **conversational withdrawals**. It's a practice that may be a little awkward at first, but will become more natural after some time, and then you won't have to think about it, you'll just benefit from it. It's imperative to realize that others are not just a conduit for you to make more progress in your life. Those who treat relationships that way are quickly revealed as self-centered solo players, and their brand will ultimately be ignored, demoted, or eliminated.

> Every conversation has equity; each word
> is worth something—cash, resources,
> influence, connection, or relationship.

Several years ago, I was looking for something new to get involved in. I called my literary agent, Joey, and asked if he knew of any new media companies. He shared about some friends who owned a small video agency called VeracityColab. It was only doing a couple hundred thousand a year in sales with three partners, but Joey shared that they were great people and had some amazing talent. This was the first conversation.

The next conversation was a phone call to one of the video agency partners to see if we could have a collective conversation. I told him I was a former agency CEO looking for something to help build, and I wanted to meet with them to see if they were open to this kind of relationship. I had resolved in my heart that this first meeting was going to be about relationship and creating value first, then see what would come out of it. You learn a lot more about people by building value *into* the relationship than you do trying to leverage things out of it. We met for about two hours, and during that time I asked a lot of questions, assessed their current business model, made some strategic recommendations, and left feeling pretty good about the meeting. They later told me they felt the same way.

A couple of weeks passed, and I hadn't heard from them. I had a branding project that I was ready to start and thought, what if I just gave this project to the video agency as a gesture to bring some teeth to the conversation? So that's what I did. It was a roughly $40,000 design project with a video. Instead of taking the business myself, I told the client I had a relationship that would be a great fit and told the guys at the video agency what it would take to make the deal happen. They went in for a single meeting and got the account. The guys called me a week later and said that they believed something was happening and wanted to talk more seriously about what it would look like for me to be working more closely with their video agency.

I figured if I contributed well to the relationship, it would end well—or in this case begin well. And that's what happened.

Long story short, we "dated" for a year, and at the end of that year I was invited in as a partner in the company. In the years ahead, in concert with the efforts of a great leadership team, we built the company into the number 1 video agency in the country, working with some of the biggest clients around the world. I can track the path of this relationship both financially and relationally directly back to a very specific and memorable conversation with my agent: "Do you happen to know anybody I can help grow?" Another conversation followed: "Would you be interested in having someone help build your company?" The rest is history.

> Intelligent conversations are progress: the
> more, the merrier; the less, the scarier.

Today at work, there are key relationships to be created, and every conversation will have value, especially if you are committed to bringing value to it. Again, think relationship before agenda. Ask any successful person and they will quickly tell you that it was the relationships that were established along the way that made the journey amazingly successful day to day, and those relationships were the catalyst for everything good that happened.

Have some meaningful, mutually focused conversations today.

15. Effective communication mandates knowing specifically who will do what by when.

One of the biggest issues hindering progress in the workplace is verbal ambiguity, or the scarcity of clear and specific communication and delegation during typical day-to-day interactions. It shows up as the daily mystery of *who* is going to do *what* by *when*. For whatever reason, leaving out much-needed specifics during communication and delegation has become standard practice because, in the busyness of it all, it's easier at times to glaze over the details and speak in generalizations—easier for the moment, that is. Although it takes a bit more work to get detailed in our conversations, delegations, and written communications, the time saved, the stress reduced, and the progress made in doing so brings value from day one. Plus, our brand becomes known as *clarity*, not obscurity.

One of the ambiguous culprits is the word *we*. *We* is a great word for the rally cry used in teams and companies.

"We will get to the number 1 position in the country!"
"We will win the next big pitch."

Beyond that, *we* can be a liability to progress where the team fails to clearly identify who will be the ones doing the work. Case in point: have you ever been in meetings where team members at the table discuss all the things that "we need to do as a company"?

"We need to improve our customer service."
"We need to improve our sales process."
"We need reengineer the workflow."

But who is *we*? The meeting moves along, topics jump around, things get lost in the exchange, and people leave the room with fragments of initiatives . . . not quite clear on who will manage the progress, get the job done, or measure the results. *Is it me, her, him, them, us, a team, a couple, Amanda, Joseph . . . ?* Who is *we*, *what* will be done, and *when* are the actual touch-points and timelines for completion . . . in detail?

The moment the *we* in our business dialogue shifts to *who* is the moment a team can take absolute responsibility for the initiatives and the people so vital to success. "We" conversations are the beginning and continuance of team chaos and the premature end of too many objectives, strategies, and tactics. By the way, moving from "we" conversations to a "who" discipline is not to subvert the team approach. On the contrary, it is the beginning of a team, the strength of a team, and the way a team gets intentional about driving individual responsibility to ensure the collective whole is served and things get done.

> Communication with specifics creates inspiration.
> Communication with ambiguity creates agitation.

"We" is a term that will create a variety of liabilities for a multitude of reasons. First, it's nearly impossible to hold "we" accountable for anything unless there are specific names and details attached to it. Secondly, "we" has become a clandestine strategy to avoid work or minimize workload, as those who live in vague "we" conversations don't have to be personally accountable for anything. "We" is also a self-protection strategy to spread our actions among a group so if something goes wrong, the blame won't land squarely on us as individuals. If we want to be well branded and well respected, it's best that we speak for ourselves and stand firmly on our convictions, not try to defray it into an obscure "we." "We" used in this way is called "responsibility risk spreading" and doesn't wear well on anyone practicing it.

Judgment, conflict, bitterness, even work-force hostility are by-products of a lack of specificity in any business environment. It only makes sense that "we" without "who" delegations will create conversations like, "Well, I thought you said you would do it," or "I wasn't told to do that," or "Wasn't so and so supposed to handle this?" Usually so much time has passed since the initial conversations that no one is quite sure of anything, and the "we" wheel keeps spinning the organization to a slow dredge.

Successful people speak with specificity and never spray conversational fog on their colleagues or teams. They lead by example, driving high performance in which everyone is on the same page and moving in a precise direction. In contrast, leaders who speak in generalities and don't drill down into the details create low-performing, high-stress cultures because of an unwillingness to consistently demand specific and complete articulations from the culture.

One often overlooked and unfortunate reality when "we" eventually becomes a specific "who" is that there's little discernment as to who the best person(s) would be for the project or initiative. Conversations move so rapidly in meetings that responsibilities are dispensed based on someone's availability of time, desire, department, and other variables that may lead to a bad choice. Rarely is there thoughtful consideration that certain gift sets from select gifted people will turn an ordinary task into extraordinary results. Often, someone with a light load will say, "I can do it," or it will be delegated to someone who has time, when in fact a person who is gifted in the task won't expend much energy or time doing the work because it falls within their gifting. Most businesses suffer from this Inappropriate Work Delegation Stress Disorder Syndrome, meaning you often have people doing work outside their talents and passion where burnout sets in or, worse, "I'm out" becomes inevitable.

The next reason why so many goals, tasks, and initiatives go bad is the lack of detail in the sharing of *what* will be done. Based on my own poor performance at times and what I have seen in corporate America, I'll assert that 60–80 percent of all "what" communications are set up to fail from the start due to a reluctance to spend time identifying and negotiating *all* the next steps. The result? You'll hear people say something like, "I told you to do it this way," or "I didn't say to do it that way," and rather than the delegator taking responsibility for their nebulous communication, they blame the other for not listening.

Fact: We'll have greater success by improving our communication so people will understand our expectations than by requiring people to get our vague generalities. People listen in direct proportion to the effectiveness of the way we articulate. But if we really want to be effective, it's best to delegate things in writing and explain in detail. Performance instantly increases, and the tension level associated with your job decreases immediately when you put things in writing. Others will take it more seriously because *you* took it more seriously.

Assumptions are another culprit in the "what" communication breakdown. We assume the other is experienced enough, or in some cases in tune enough, to get it with basic, brief, or fly-by communication. When it comes to conveying what you want, don't assume anything; be detailed, be clear, review points, confirm understanding, and encourage excellence in every communication. If people around me are not following through for me on a regular basis, I'll always look in the mirror and reflect on how I'm communicating—or more to the point, *not* communicating.

The third place where specificity is needed is in timelines and deadlines, which are often the lifelines of business: the *when*. For some reason there seems to be a pervasive fear to simply tell someone exactly when you need something done. We use timid phrases like "Get it to me when you can, or ASAP" or "Get it to me next week sometime" or "Sometime tomorrow will be okay."

For obvious reasons, these milquetoast time frames bite us almost every time. They also throw awkwardness into relationships with our co-workers that really doesn't need to be there. For example, has someone ever given you a delegation to do something and said, "When you can get around to it is fine"? A couple of days later, they come up frantically assuring you they told you they needed it that day. It will happen millions of times today—and millions will be unduly frustrated, angry, hurt, or stressed by their own volition.

> You won't find ASAP in any pro's language; you'll find requests are made with specific timelines. ASAP isn't a commitment, it's confusion.

It's just as important for us to draw out the *who*, *what*, and *when* specifics from people who make vague requests of us as it is for us to be specific with others. It creates accountability and capitalizes on our true performance potential and our most important asset: time. Nobody said specific communication was easy. However, the price we pay for allowing nebulous communication to permeate our conversations is steep, resulting in extra work, increased anxiety, greater complexity, and dozens of unnecessary negative outcomes.

Specificity in communication is not so much about what you have to do, but who you are. It's a discipline of integrating clarity as a core value so others can be clear in relationship with you. You develop your character and your way of being with people while measuring the results you attain . . . specifically! If your results are less than acceptable, you'll be willing to look at your role and be accountable for the results as a responsible professional, not a victim.

Be more specific about "who" and "what" by "when" today, and watch how things become easier, more enjoyable, and productive.

16. Regardless of professional position, everyone is in sales—the consistent process of convincing people that things should be one way or the other.

If you think about it, any business is an ongoing series of negotiations. We don't always see it that way, but today when you go to work, someone will be trying to get you to see something their way or you will be in a process of getting others to see things your way. Therefore, we are all sales professionals—it's just that some are selling products and services and the rest of us are selling our ideas, direction, delegation, responsibilities, and things that are necessary for daily progress. The idea that business and all that happens in it is due to what you negotiate is something to subscribe to and a skill to perfect.

Even those of us who would never label ourselves as sales professionals, aka *negotiators*, negotiate nonstop at work, at home with our families, at the store with the clerk, at the service center with the general manager, with vendors, investors . . . the list goes on. In essence, pretty much everyone is on the other end of our negotiating ability, whether we're trying to get into a better position at work or out of a speeding ticket on the street.

The foundation of getting better at negotiating (aka *persuading, influencing, controlling, directing, selling,* and *moving*) with others is to first acknowledge the fact that *you are a negotiator*. One cannot improve on what one hasn't identified. Next is to understand that *negotiator* can be a noble position if we are willing to bring excellence and care to every person in every transaction. We all know there's skill in negotiation, but it also has a heartbeat at the foundation.

Although there are several schools of thought on negotiation strategies and tactics, I take the approach to first care, then move to skills, strategies, and tactics.

> Making sure others are winning in business has a way of simplifying business. It removes the energy and the stress of scheming, manipulating, and coercing and creates a peaceful process with a win-win as the ultimate measure of victory.

So how does "care" move from an abstract concept to a relevant tool in negotiation? First, before you enter into a negotiation of any size or type, take some time to contemplate and write down what a win would look like for the person on the other side. Also consider what a loss for them might be. It's amazing how clear the big picture becomes when you step into someone else's shoes to see and feel their side in the context of what you want. It helps you to see all the components of a negotiation in a single view instead of just your own parts, and allows you to engage with a sensitivity the other side will immediately appreciate. This is the beginning of a great negotiation.

Some time ago, my business partner and one of my executives pitched me on a lucrative online gaming play. My partner's father was one of the top poker players in the world, and we had inroads to the space that would have made introductions and getting meetings all but done. After they shared the idea with me, I stepped away to consider the ramifications of getting into the gambling business. It took about thirty minutes of concentrated thought to call another meeting and share my thoughts. They were pretty passionate about it, and thus began the negotiation. Knowing we were all Christian guys, had high core values, and valued relationship, I walked into their office and said this near verbatim.

> Guys, obviously this sounds like a pretty amazing opportunity and a very profitable one, but after some thought I want you to consider a few things. The first is that today no less than a hundred people will lose their homes because of gambling problems; out of those hundred or so, fifty marriages will probably be broken apart if they haven't been already. I'm guessing at least a couple dozen in the next few months will become homeless due to losing everything because of gambling problems. And this may seem like a stretch, but I believe in the next year

or so, many people will be beaten severely, and some even murdered, because they couldn't pay their gambling debt due to their addiction.

I didn't have to raise my voice or get overly emotional—I just delivered something that I thought would be relevant for them to consider. We went back and forth for a while, and at the end of the conversation I asked them to consider the simplicity of what I said in my opening statements as a very clear and present reality. I concluded by saying that this was not something that we needed to be involved in to get where we wanted to go. And as a final emphasis of my position I shared this very calmly: "If you guys decide to go down that road, I'll understand, but it won't be a road I'll be going down, so we need to figure out a way to buy me out of the business."

A couple weeks later, we collectively and permanently stopped the initiative and proceeded with our business. Although it seems like I was playing hardball, the intent of my heart was to care for theirs. I knew in the moment they were seeing more dollar signs than danger signs. The negotiation ended well because I knew they would opt for the win for their characters over the win for their wallets.

> Chances of successful negotiations that don't
> move toward win-win are thin-thin.

Emotions play a big part in negotiation, and if you're prepared, you can bring the negotiation down to a relaxed level that facilitates an atmosphere where everyone is thinking rationally and peacefully. Whether you are negotiating or selling yourself into or out of something, care is the catalyst responsible for making things work and is the driving force for knowing what is important to others. Thinking through what those things might be and starting negotiations by asking what is important to others takes them off the offensive or defensive and puts them in a position where they become collaborative. Given enough care toward the other, they'll often begin the process of thinking on your behalf, which is where negotiations don't just create results, they create lasting relationships that go far beyond the negotiation.

◀ **In all things, negotiate with care today.** ▶

17. We are not known for the intentions we have, we are known for the differences we make.

If you gave a colleague a critical delegation—one that if not completed would have serious repercussions—and you asked them if they could get it done, what would you rather hear? "Well it will be my intention to get it done." Or, "Don't worry about a thing, it will be done; you can be certain of that."

Ever hold a good intention in your hand? Ever try to buy or trade something with an intention? Although the emotional value of intentions may be a good feeling, and we appreciate pure motives, they have no tangible value to those around us. By themselves, intentions have little impact on our brand, promotion, progress . . . even growth. Some choose to live in a world where just the effort alone is valued as good enough, where everyone gets first place because they played in the game. The problem with that is once they come back from a float in the clouds, the only place they land is fantasyland, where everyone depends on the abstract and the only real thing is uncertainty and stagnancy.

> If you want to know the value of an intention versus a result, just try writing someone a check for an intention.

In today's world the measure of our value comes from the difference we make in the physical universe, not necessarily what exists in our heart or our intentions. It's not a cold, callous position; results are what people need today—not empty promises, broken commitments, or (as innocent as they sound) intentions. In fact, in high-performing environments, everyone is expected to be intentional and there is no brand value in claiming that trait. Bottom line: The words "I intend to get it done" should never come from our mouths, and if they come from the mouths of others we should ask for a more resolute commitment. Our value to others rests on our ability to be consistent in the results we promise to others and the differences we actually make.

Make sure your intentions manifest into making a difference today.

18. Never underestimate the damage that occurs by breaking commitments that appear insignificant.

During the course of a work month, you may be asked or may task yourself to complete something quite substantial. But that's not an everyday occurrence, or even a weekly one. Instead, what comprises our typical work life are dozens of ongoing small commitments, from "I'll get this to you by 2 PM," to "I'll be at the meeting on time," to "I'll call you back on that." The small things exist in great numbers, every day, everywhere . . . and they never stop coming.

We all know there are ramifications when we break a BIG commitment. But breaking the small, casually made ones is among those practices we believe we can get away with by crafting creative excuses, charming manipulation, or simply just blowing them off. It's as if we think breaking these small, fly-by commitments isn't vital to our reputation or relationships—perhaps because it's the norm: "everyone's doing it."

However, when we do keep every commitment we make, people take note. Trust gets forged when absolute dependability is present. In contrast, the buildup of small commitments not kept will kill our brand, and sometimes our character, silently and permanently.

> Keeping our word in the small things will ensure
> we get invited into more of the big things.

People have the capacity to further our position in our life and career, and those we work with pay closer attention to the small things than we think; they know our commitment level will often be revealed in how we handle the details—the little things and the implied promises we make. The problem arises when we either don't keep track of the small commitments we make, they slip through the cracks, we fail to have a good reminder system, or we simply don't care enough to keep them. It's a choice we make to be "on it"—on all of the small things—and it creates an impression when we make all types of commitments (from casual to serious) and keep them with total consistency. It shows we care, it shows we value being organized, and it ultimately shows we can be trusted with bigger things.

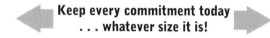

**Keep every commitment today
. . . whatever size it is!**

19. True success is a pace—not a race.

Having been CEO of a large ad agency, I've worked with a diversity of people over the years. Everyone who worked in our agency was capable of doing the job and doing it well because of a screening process that was tantamount to being vetted for a senior-level operative position in a highly classified government environment. We put our candidates through a gauntlet of exercises with various people and a mix of serious challenges because we realized there are no bad hires, just bad hiring practices. We hired with great care because we didn't want to taint the culture with capable people who were missing the human attributes that make a company a peaceful, collaborative, and amazing place to be.

The one characteristic of the employees we hired that we weren't able to see clearly in the interview process was how they would move through a week's work. We had to wait to see how that panned out by watching how they engaged. Some people we hired moved at a pace that was methodical, leaving room for them to engage in relationship-building conversations and offering them ample time and bandwidth to help others. They had a sense of peace about them, no fear-driven behavior, and they were present enough in the environment to catch things others might miss. We appreciated these people greatly. They were an asset that saved the day on more than one occasion because they chose to move at the pace of awareness on the projects they were working on. Their helpful disposition and their awareness and insight positioned them as well liked, and they were first to be considered for promotions, raises, and other forms of commendation.

> If you try to reach goals too fast, you'll often get busted for exceeding the greed limit.

On the other hand, some people came on board and did their job well, but that's all they did. It's like they walked in the door, climbed on the hamster wheel and didn't get off until the day was over. Their entire agenda was to get the hamster wheel spinning as fast as they could while being careful not to fall off, slow down, or make mistakes. They did their job, which was noticeable. But what was more noticeable than anything else was their focus on themselves. They moved at such a quick pace that they missed out on the many rewards of giving into a culture and people that went beyond their job description. This archetype would move so fast they became invisible to the eye of others. That's what happens when you isolate in plain sight and stay too focused on your own world. It gets lonely, empty, and the hamster wheel burns you out until it flings you off into who knows what.

> Slow down a bit. Good things happen there.

There's no other way to put it: there's a real beauty about those who move at a pace of awareness and cultural sensitivity. Within the confines of their crazy workday they see the colleague struggling with the client, project, or goal—or if even more aware, the marriage, the problem at home—and step in to offer to help or be a listening ear. Being an asset in business and living in the purpose of who we are beyond our job is what creates a great reputation at work, not to mention it makes a great human being. It will take any day from being tolerable to being enjoyable and makes getting out of bed in the morning a more valiant endeavor. This goal will have you showing up to work and thinking to yourself, *Who can I encourage today? Who can I make laugh or bring a cup of coffee to? Who may need my help or need me to listen?* As I shared before, the small things make a huge difference. And the reason is . . . drumroll please . . . *nobody's doing them.* Everyone is just too busy busting tail on the hamster wheel, pushing maximum speed, looking straight ahead with no distractions.

Don't be a hamster. Move at the pace of awareness and surprise others with some attentiveness today.

20. Sometimes a trip to the cemetery can bring life to our brand.

Right now, as a brand, you're carrying a certain amount of emotional baggage. We all carry some at any given time, but the goal in your work is to move lightly, nimbly, and with luggage to go places, not baggage to slow you down. Your baggage may have been acquired as a result of something that happened today, a recent event, or perhaps several things that built up over a long period of time.

Emotional baggage compounds as a result of life itself, and at any given time we can be carrying a few ounces or a ton—all of which acts as weight that impacts our success and the way others experience us. Complacency, poor performance, and life confusion as well as things like catastrophic events, relationship breakdowns, and career failures accumulate; some of them are self-inflicted and with others we had no choice. Baggage can come from just about anywhere and ends up in the most important part of our brand—our presence.

Presence is what others experience of us when we enter *their presence*, their space, or a room of people. We can't escape the attribute of presence; we carry it with us and it affects the outcome of every conversation, meeting, presentation, and interview. Since it influences everything, managing our emotional weight and the persona of our presence is key to our emotional impact on others.

> The impact of our words is often determined
> by the presence we carry as we say them.

A while back, I met with a friend of mine who is one of the top business coaches in the country. I was at a place in my career where I wasn't certain what was next and realized I'd been in that place for several years. Emotional baggage was draped around me like a thick, wet curtain, and I could feel its presence daily. So could others I worked and lived with. I told my friend a bit of what was going on, and we came up with a list of things that just weren't working in my life and my career—things like attitudes, beliefs, events, behaviors, and relationships. Then he said the strangest thing to me:

> I'd like you to expand on your list, and once completed, print a copy, go to a cemetery with a small shovel, find a place in the corner, crumple up the list, and bury it—and not just in a shallow grave. Bury it deep, so you'll remember you did. These things need to die.

It turned out to be such a profound exercise that the following week when I was mentoring a young man who had amassed some mental, emotional, and relational baggage in his career, I asked him to do the same thing. After completion, the young man emailed me:

> Hello Dean,
>
> Just following up quickly to let you know I did that cemetery exercise I committed to do. Wasn't sure what to expect, but it was life changing. Glad you convinced me it was necessary!

> A mind is much like a hard drive; free up some memory by deleting some old useless files—it makes room for the new files you create.

Whether it's a trip to the cemetery or throwing a list into a fireplace, there's something very special about the idea of doing something physical and tangible with that baggage rather than continuing to allow it to mess with your mind and infect your presence. Unfortunately, casually rethinking baggage and making small adjustments doesn't have the finality necessary to deal with it once and for all. Whatever the ceremony, if you will, give it a try from time to time.

If the emotional weight you are experiencing is greater than what may be helped with a symbolic exercise (which I would try regardless),

I recommend getting help with the issues that are keeping you from having the kind of presence and brand you want, and do it sooner rather than later. We've all got stuff, but when heavy baggage is dealt with, it transforms into light luggage that enables us to travel to new places, create new experiences with new people, and facilitate better results.

Write down what's not working and bury it today!

21. Our performance will always be measured in percentages.

A friend of mine told me once that everything in life was reflected by a percentage. I disagreed. He asked, "How sure are you, honestly?" The more I thought about it, the more I realized I was about 80 percent sure. It got me thinking that when I was young and thought I knew everything, I was 99.9 percent naïve. When I started a business, I was about 75 percent sure I'd succeed. When a project failed, I'd generally only put 60 percent into it. When I got pulled over for speeding, I was about 95 percent truthful and still got the ticket. Take any verb, such as *perform, care, work, feel, try, speak, think, commit,* and so on. Then consider that we have a way of fooling ourselves into believing we do them at full power, 100 percent of the time. At times in our careers, we defend the 100-percent-effort position as if our lives depend on it.

Know this: People, teams, and departments around us aren't fooled by our biased view of our own performance. They've got us pegged at a lower percentage that is pretty accurate—give or take a few percent. But we shouldn't always have to rely on others to measure our potential; we should own the responsibility to know the level of commitment we are giving to our work by paying closer attention to the percentages.

> The truth of our work performance should never scare us. What should scare us and send fear into the marrow of our bones is ignoring the truth about how we are really doing at work.

A life in which we are honest with ourselves—such as, "I got fired at my job because I gave about 50 percent to it," or, "I didn't get the raise because I've been cruising at 75 percent"—is the beginning of real growth. The "I'm always at 100 percent myth" assumes perfection and leaves no room for us to contemplate how we can improve, mature, be more valuable to those around us, and have a greater sense of fulfillment. It's an illusion that ignores the progressive growth we can be at ease with—as imperfect humans, growing, learning, and acknowledging our progress.

Improve a few percent to experience the most today.

22. Sleep is essential to energy. Energy is essential to your work and brand. Bedtime shouldn't be dread time.

As a CEO of several companies during my career, I've heard the excuse of poor sleep used for projects not delivered up to standard or presentations lacking energy and results, and of course, late arrivals at work. I've used it myself. However, that doesn't change the fact that we are responsible for getting great sleep and bringing our A-game to work. An ongoing good night's sleep is critical to life success.

> Better performance at work helps us sleep better at night. Better sleep at night helps us perform better at work.

Bedtime is an interesting time. It opens the gate of the mind like no other time of day. Just when everything is about to shut down, the mind can accelerate into a maze of mental inventions, worries, and question marks; this is not the ideal time for that, as our mind is too tired to fight that kind of battle. I struggled with this for years until I decided there was no value there and this was not the time or place to fight, but to surrender and sleep. The truth is I needed the rest, and the time to be working out my life was during the day when I could contemplate, plan, log next steps, and consult others if needed. I simply proclaimed that nighttime is the time *I get to rest*, and I gave it up. I came to believe that I'd be more effective the next day with a good night's sleep.

Energy, clear thinking, and healthy life performance come from a place of rest, not restlessness, and we are entitled to that rest, knowing that all the equipping we need for tomorrow will be more accessible the next day with a good night's sleep. Because we sleep for around 33 percent of our lives, it makes sense to learn best practices for what to think and do before our head hits the pillow. Then we can hit tomorrow performing and not yawning.

Give yourself permission to rest tonight and wake up a brand new you.

23. True listening will occur in the details of our attention.

If you want to be a brand at your company or organization that is trusted, respected, and appreciated, *listen closely*. I'll discuss listening in this book from a few angles, as it is one of the most critical business skills there is. But attentive listening—listening that brings us to a new level of understanding, intelligence, and productivity in business situations—is always under threat due to a mind that is trying to keep pace managing all the moving parts of our work lives. The result is that we end up listening in fragments and miss important conversational components essential to insight, only to have the fragmented listening assault our progress and put our brand back at the starting gate.

Listening is a commitment we make to honor others and stay within the confines of the conversation so we can be a resource to optimize the exchange and not hinder it. There is such a predictable emotional emptiness that occurs when we disconnect in conversations, it's a wonder we ever do it. But we do it because we place more importance on ourselves and our needs and wants than on the speaker, and that is no way to build our brand in a relationship, or to build a relationship in general. In contrast, it's a sure way to destroy it—quickly.

There is an emotional and relational richness and respect that's revealed when we practice undistracted listening, and it shows up immediately on the faces of those we are listening to. We receive the best communication from others when they know we are honoring their words and their time. In turn, they will respect your time and honor you back in the process.

This doesn't mean we have to listen to those who are inclined to drone on forever. We hold the keys to the direction and duration of conversations by what we request from them. If there are those who have a propensity for a velocity of verbosity, set aside a time to tell them what style or nature of communication works best for you. Some people benefit from conversations that are highly detail oriented, while others need just the bottom line; it's our responsibility to share what works best for us if communication is moving toward a state of breakdown.

The truth is, intentional listening can be a great deal of fun, and you'll be pleased with the social brilliance you'll acquire by practicing a laser focus when someone is talking. Even those looking in on a focused conversation can spot a great listener from across the room.

> **Wisdom is found in slowing down enough to really listen.**

Here's listening defined in its purest form:

- Listening is focused eye contact—**respect.**
- Listening is hearing, considering, and meditating on every word spoken—**wisdom.**
- Listening is scanning between the words to hear that which the other might be too uncomfortable to say—**insight.**
- Listening is not drifting, but staying in tune, patiently waiting for the other to finish before speaking—**intelligence.**
- Listening is asking for clarification and understanding ("What I'm hearing you say is . . ." or "Tell me more")—**curiosity.**
- Listening is not thinking of what you will say next, but responding to what is said—**productivity.**
- Listening is acknowledging the other has had a different upbringing and different influences, and is in need of being communicated to in a way that works for them—**sensitivity.**

This is the beginning of relationship, and this is the acceleration of your brand. By the way, if you're not doing *all* of this, you are *not* listening—or are merely listening to a percentage of the message.

Hearing is a function of the senses;
listening is a commitment of the heart.
Listen from the heart today.

24. True professionals see problems as provisions and obstacles as opportunities.

Every breakdown or dose of adversity you encounter in work relationships is an opportunity to grow in abundant ways. Our workplaces tend to be intense, dynamic places with a diversity of people, cultures, backgrounds, personalities, and quirks. These human factors can make relationships a challenge, a flat-out nightmare, or *a great opportunity*. But how, when, and where we deal with them can make all the difference. One of the attributes that will make your brand equity attractive in the grand scheme of your work life is your ability to take a difficult relationship and spin it into reconciliation with consistency and deliberateness. In contrast, those who choose to allow conflict to fester will simply prolong the suffering or usher the relationship into such a state of turmoil that someone eventually has to go. That leaves a 50/50 chance of you being ousted simply because either you or the other party is unwilling to engage to kill the conflict.

> Peace is not found in the absence of difficulty but in embracing the value you know is within difficulty.

At my video agency, VeracityColab, one of our core values is to "charge storms like a buffalo." The premise is that when a storm comes, most animals will run away from the storm, and the storm will follow them. On the other hand, the buffalo in its infinite buffalo brain power chooses to charge the storm by running straight into it. The buffalo knows that in doing so the storm will pass quickly over it, following the other animals (adding perhaps a little spite and laughter to its forthcoming dryness and comfort). Relational breakdowns in companies are the same way. If we take immediate steps to remedy breakdowns by calling a conversation to address the issues, the storm can pass quickly rather than build up bitterness and resentment.

> To postpone a relationship breakdown not
> solved will not get that problem resolved.

There's no "one size fits all" formula for reconciliation, but I've discovered in every relationship I've been in where there's been a breakdown, I've contributed a certain amount to the problem by either causing it, contributing to it, or allowing it to occur. Regardless, I approach the table with some acknowledgment of my part in the mess. If I lead by stating the problem as a mutual problem, and I let the other party know that I'd like to resolve it, that will typically create a safe space for the other to do the same. And even if they don't admit wrongdoing, your accounting for your role in the conflict creates a more trusted place for them to receive the feedback on their role in the breakdown at the right time—especially if the intention is to improve the relationship, not just to be right.

Stressed relationships that go through a reconciliation process early on end up being more durable and rewarding than those left unattended. When negativities take root and the dysfunctional behaviors continue, the problem is exacerbated.

Got a problem with a co-worker? Go be the brand of reconciliation and progress today.

25. Every thought can be reengineered from destructive to constructive in about thirty seconds.

Ever notice how your mental currency is pretty much spent by the end of each workday? Evening words can dwindle to near necessity and thoughts scramble sluggishly at any effort to assemble them; the next thing you know, you wake the following morning and presto, your mental bank account is near full once again. Why does our brain energy dwindle so quickly? One reason is the all-too-common self-destructive stories we allow into our head about basic things: *How badly did the meeting go? Will the presentation fail? Do I have relevancy? Am I good enough? Will I get the deal? Is this the right approach? Do they like me?* The problem with these self-inflicted, mentally manufactured self-assaults is that we lose precious intellectual capital with every negative thought.

> It takes several times the mental capacity to invent a bad outcome than it does to prepare for a great outcome.

The process of reengineering our thought life to install new confidence in our lives begins with math: it takes less time to invent strategy, integrate planning, and originate a positive viewpoint or attitude than it does to multiply the garbage created by an undisciplined mind. Neural pathways form in our mind based on the thoughts we have (as if they were grooves), and the more thoughts we think along the same lines, the deeper the grooves become and the more consistent the thought flow . . . whether positive or negative.

It may sound sophomoric, but as thoughts that you'd rather be without enter into your mind, hold them still for a moment and say, "Not so fast. Let's have a little chat before you go any further." This is the process of changing the conversation we have with ourselves; it is as tactical as it is practical, and it will provide enough mental bandwidth for a fully energized day, not a half-energized let-down toward the end. Your mind is a tricky thing. It can unnerve and swerve you when all it should do is serve you.

Grab a few mental inventions and reinvent them today.

26. Past successes are a good thing . . . until they're not.

Confession time: I have rested on the successes of my past, thinking they would fuel my future, when in fact all they fueled was an insecure need to be sought-after while I fantasized about life working on cruise control. Life doesn't work that way. Truth is, *that* whimsical paradigm stifled my momentum, weakened my balance sheet, and showed me that the value found in past successes pales in contrast to the worth found through hard work and a clear vision in present moments.

> Any woman who is resting on previous successes should get a "history-ectomy." Any man who is resting on previous successes should get a "past-ectomy." Sorry, couldn't help myself. ☺

The good news is, my paradigm of resting on past success has shifted the reality and "what's next" trumps "what was" any day of the week. Rather than expecting the phone to ring, I'm working on causing it to ring, *and it's ringing*. It's embarrassing to confess such a thing, but if I can spare anyone the grief of a career-hindering, emotionally taxing episode, season, or decade then so be it. There's something to be said for staying in a rhythm while we work and having it fueled by our commitment to what we do today, not what happened yesterday.

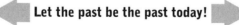 **Let the past be the past today!**

27. Using too many words when we write is a direct hit on our brand. That's the long and short of it.

In today's content-saturated world of way too many words, verbosity seems to be alive and well and brevity seems to be a lost art.

> ## Just what does "brevity" mean in the realm of business communications?

brev·i·ty: *[brev-i-tee] noun.* **Standard definition:** the quality of expressing much in fewer words. **brevity**—author redefined. 1. The principle of communicating smarter, not harder and stronger, not longer. 2. Velocity instead of verbosity. The difference between communicating and aggravating. 3. A clear indicator of excellence, intelligence, and competence. 4. What people want, appreciate, and respond to. 5. The only truly effective way to communicate these days. 6. A clear way to value people and improve your communication . . . written or verbal.

Knowing our brand is the emotional connection others have with us, there is an inherent opportunity to do things that make people feel better and more productive. One of the indicators of how much one cares for those in their sphere of influence manifests in how clearly and concisely they communicate to them. It's the "we know you're busy, so here's the bottom line" approach. Those who employ the discipline of brevity in their communications are considered a breath of fresh air among the verbose. Communication is primarily designed to provoke, persuade, and direct, and if people today understood that, we'd have a lot more focused and valuable content around and people would read materials more often. The need for straight-to-the-point communications will wear in, never out.

> In the competition to communicate something you want others to read, lesser generally wins.

How we write in business is of great importance whether we deem ourselves writers or not. When people read an email, internal memo, article, blog post, or presentation that gets straight to the point, the perception the reader gains from the writer is that they are intelligent, articulate, caring, wise, and straightforward. In contrast, when a reader encounters something with an abundance of content but no consideration toward brevity, the frustration, stress, and discouragement sets in—as well as, "Oh, it's *them* again."

The formula for more effective writing is founded on this: writing with brevity will force better thinking, and accepting the challenge of condensing all content is a great discipline. Identify the most relevant, compelling, and true points you need to get across, and focus on those and those only. This is the platform for brevity-based communications.

> As for word count in written communication, the fewer the better and the better write fewer.

Structurally, consider that your main messages should be communicated clearly in the headlines, subheads, floating quotes, or callouts. People are scanners, and if they pick up value by reading the standouts, they'll drill down to the details. If not, they're gone. For example, when people pick up a copy of *Shift Your Thinking for Success*, generally they will look at some of the titles on the pages, and read some of the callouts highlighted; if they like what they see they'll give the book a shot. If the big type doesn't grab, the book stays on the shelf and the supporting content is never read. People zero in on the obvious content first. So the goal of any piece of written communication should be to communicate the value or main point in just the headlines, subheads, and supporting visuals or callouts. If the message captivates, your chances of them digging into the message are multiplied and people will appreciate the lead-in.

It's not always bad to write long copy, if it's the right project and there's a predictable audience. Comprehensive copy is welcomed when the goal is to educate or sell to a niche audience who wants in-depth reading on a certain topic. But keep in mind, this is still no excuse to write without sensitivity: the recipient has a life that would be well served if you convey the message succinctly. Tools such as white papers, books, ebooks, and advertorials are a few pieces that allow for more detail—relevant and provocative factual detail.

Here's an analogy. If you can hold up a sign for the man who doesn't see the bus coming that says STOP OR DIE or a sign that says EXCUSE ME, KIND SIR, COULD YOU PLEASE SPARE A MOMENT? I'D LIKE TO TAKE THIS OPPORTUNITY TO SHARE WITH YOU THAT THERE'S A . . . BAM!!!, you'll be supporting the revolution of brevity. And if you strategically minimize your quantity of words in communication, you'll have more time, notice improved receptivity from everyone who comes in contact with you, and reap an increase in effectiveness.

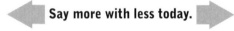 **Say more with less today.**

28. In your not-so-spare time, will you do what you want to do? Or regret that you didn't do what you wanted?

We do things outside of work—hobbies, passions, and activities—not so much for what they get us, but what they *install* into us. We all have at least one thing we've wanted to do for a long time. Shelved, postponed, or languishing in stall-mode, goals like writing, art, hiking, joining a gym, reading, or building something are collecting dust in such volume they can barely be seen. Now look at your calendar. Not enough time, is there! Or is there? A quick look at current time expenditures reveals things that are robbing you of the time to do something more meaningful—you know, that thing you've been *wanting* to do and know you'd be really good at if you committed to it.

> Television is anthrax to the soul, Novocain to the mind, Valium to the body, and arsenic to the spirit.

If you take a moment to design your life from the end of it backward, you'll see there is only so much time left. A quick study of the time remaining can have you looking at your current time allocation with the level of urgency that will mandate rearranging the blocks of time—*but only if you look.*

I used to think I had all the time in the world, but at the time of writing this book my life has thirty-five, maybe forty-five years left. When I realized that, it demanded a conversation for something I'd wanted to get back to—my artwork. Hadn't touched it in decades, but of course I saw the latest-and-greatest TV series as an obvious "add" to my life. Ha! For me the exchange was less TV time for more creative time—an easy switch, especially after I hit my stride. And now it's hard to imagine watching too much TV (aka Taking Vision). But the real value of doing something you love on the side is that it adds to your perspective of how you see your work and life. It provides a bit of rest for your mind, refuels and balances you, and gives you greater joy so you can contend with the demands of work with greater ease and energy.

Consider "that thing" as a replacement part for something you really won't miss today.

29. Currently, you're building two brands in life: one offline and (just as important) one online.

I recently received a call from an entrepreneur regarding a *single* complaint about his performance that was posted on a notable review site by an unhappy party. I'll remain confidential about the name of the review site, but it rhymes with HELP! Although he tried diligently to resolve the matter prior to post, that single online rant turned into a multitude of financial, relational, and emotional issues. Another friend shared that information about a lawsuit they were involved in (and won) ended up online and cost them immediate revenue and important long-term opportunities. Whether a review site, blog post, or social-channel comment, a single online post can affect our personal brand. From a simple hiccup we can move to not getting more business, not getting the job or the promotion, and all the way to bankruptcy. Once damaging reviews, degrading content, and less-than-flattering comments attached to our brand are online . . . *they're up*, and getting them down can be tedious, emotionally taxing, and expensive.

> One breakdown in your online presence is like a branding iron that stamps on your forehead "I'm a risk!"

Here are a few key things to think about when considering your online brand.

1. As a baseline, conduct a thorough search of "you" online. Go deep in the page count, searching text, videos, and images to see what's there so you get a pulse of your personal online brand. A simple search can reveal a sigh of relief or a ton of grief. Set a quarterly reminder to do a quick checkup.

2. Own this truth: providing status-quo performance to those in your world is dead, not to mention dangerous; you're gambling with potential online repercussions. Safeguard yourself by not just doing the job you promised, but going beyond what is expected of you and building in a couple of nice surprises along the way. Pleasant surprises accelerate and increase the number of positive posts.

3. When you have a conflict in a relationship or on a project, don't wait to resolve it; handle it quick, like your pants are on fire, and bring it to an amicable finish. People typically post in the heat of the moment and sometimes regret their hostility, but by that time it may be too late. Hoping a business problem of any kind will just go away is a bad strategy, especially considering that the opportunity to harm your reputation is ever present. Have a plan in place for if (more like *when*) a complaint gets posted. As a first measure, you can contact the person who placed the post and try to bring it to a resolution, as they may revise or remove the quote on their own if you can work it out.

4. Lastly, be cognizant of what you post online, what you view online, and who you connect with online. Employers and professionals alike are using social channels (legally or not) as part of their review and interview process, and the brand you build online is of equal importance to your offline brand. Knowing several people high up in human resources, I hear stories of how social presence often tells more about a person than their interview—and many times, the determining factor for whether someone got the job, the account, the whatever, was something the interviewer saw online, either good or bad.

> I imagine someday that every website you ever visited, every post you ever posted, or every post posted about you will be available by putting in a credit card number and hitting "get report." Hmm!

As technologies continually evolve to track, measure, and innovate ways to gather information on both companies and individuals, our exposure to more detailed profiles on our habits and activities will become more available to the mainstream. I find this to be a troubling reality, but in doing some research, it's already quite unnerving what people can discover with the paid subscriptions and online services available today.

The best course of action is always preventative. How you service those you work with and for, handle complaints, deliver on your commitments, and manage your social channels is the foundation of your reputation online and off, and the only way to predictably minimize chances of potential brand damage.

Do a little digging, thinking, and planning related to your online brand today.

30. The value of our time is often found in the quality of people we spend it with and the way in which we use that time.

A friend of mine was at the Dallas airport, snapped a shot of my first book, *Shift Your Thinking*, and sent me an email saying that I was "in good company." My book was positioned right next to Dave Ramsey's new book. I was indeed in good company, and I'm sure sales were influenced because of it. That got me thinking about who we connect with, how we engage with them, and the value therein. As the old saying goes, our growth is often determined by the books we read, the people we meet, and the choices we make. As for the people we spend time with or choose not to, there are several variables that influence whether we grow through those important choices.

First, make it a focus to spend time with people you are philosophically and ethically aligned with—people with the same passion, energy level, and desire to achieve. They don't have to be in the same profession (though it helps), they just need to be cut from the same cloth so when conversing, you can hit the ground relating, brainstorming, and sharing ideas that will have impact on your life. The emotional capital gained from each exchange will leave you more fulfilled, energized, and directed—not to mention the ancillary values that can come from these meetings such as opportunities, connections, and more.

Stretch yourself to attain meetings with thought leaders or mentors who you may think are unavailable because they are too busy. Successful people are successful because they can manage time, and they will have time for you if you humbly ask for their help over a "free" lunch or coffee. I've asked complete strangers who have businesses twenty times the size of mine for advice, and I haven't been turned down yet. That still surprises me, but it's true. People generally like to help, and the value from these conversations—some of which turn into relationships—is priceless.

It's a valuable practice (and essential to your bandwidth) to say no to attending meetings if they are not urgent when other matters are pressing or you're in goal mode. There are times in life when we have bandwidth and times we legitimately don't, and when you don't, decline the meetings that don't move the needle on critical mass. When my time is limited and people I'm on the phone with say, "Hey, let's get together and catch up soon," I often say something like, "Let's catch up now—tell me what's going on." Then we continue to talk, and I'm updated without travel and meeting time. This leaves more time for things that need to get done. If they are resolute about meeting face-to-face, I will generally say, "Reach out to me after [my critical time] and we'll get something on the calendar." Most of the time they don't reach out—so in short, you'll find out if it was really that important.

> The intentionality we have when we are with people will determine the value derived from and delivered into those relationships.

Have different conversations. At a conference once, I heard poet David Whyte mention that a courageous conversation is one that is different from the one you've currently been having or have had many times before. When meeting with others, challenge yourself to stay away from recycled conversations. Although these conversations get the things we say to sound as good as possible, they rarely reflect the "current us." Instead of growing us, recycled conversations can shrink us into a repetitive chat that even we get sick of hearing.

Lastly, spend a few minutes thinking about how you can add value to the person you're meeting with. Consider their life, circumstances, and career, and you'll come up with forms of connection, encouragement, or conversation that impact their circumstances. A little goes a long way.

Take inventory of who you're hanging with and add a few greats to the list today.

31. How we connect with the words we speak determines how others connect with our words.

Getting better at communication—whether spoken or written—is serious progress. At some point in your career your audience will get larger—in some cases suddenly—so improving your ability to resonate while speaking to a group or an audience is among the more important tools for present and future successes. It's also a lot of fun when we do it well. But what does it mean to "do it well"?

Consider some of the speakers you've heard but have left underwhelmed, feeling like they gave a decent speech but lacked authenticity and seemed like they were using more of a going-through-the-motions approach. Although they were verbalizing, there was a disconnect where the words were being spoken; the conviction trailed miles behind the words and never caught up. It's as if the speaker practiced the heart and soul right out of the talk. It's pretty common these days.

> No one needs another "going through the motions" presentation, talk, or speech. We don't need to be held captive, only to listen to a flesh-covered tape recorder.

Recently, I went to hear a speaker who is a published author and CEO. He had 60,000 employees in his company, and I was all but certain his accomplishments must have grounded him to be real, purposeful in his approach, and passionate about his talk, so I looked forward to the speech. Prior to his presentation, a middle-aged Taiwanese man shared his brief story of success for ten minutes in a broken dialect. The audience was riveted, cheered, and was grateful to hear his story—but more important, to hear his heart. Following that, the CEO got up and delivered a pasty, disconnected talk for forty-five minutes that felt like eating a tasteless cake. The room was virtually silent except for the occasional mercy laugh at his attempted jokes. I'm not sure what they paid him to speak, but we all paid a price to listen beyond the money we paid to get in.

Fact: Manufactured eloquence and practiced polish in public speaking is dying a slow death, as is data regurgitation and overly slick delivery. Whenever we speak, it's wise to note that people aren't necessarily moved, nor do they obtain value, solely by what we say or how well we say it. The value we create comes mostly through our way of being when we're sharing. It's about the posture of our hearts and how much we care for those before us—as well as our commitment to be prepared and genuine, and to connect with our audience—that will breathe life into the words we share.

Compelling and effective speakers

- stay grounded in what they are committed to cause in the hearts and minds of their audience
- care less about what the speaker evaluation sheet will soon reveal, and care more about changing lives and creating progress
- are willing to take risks and are more inclined to challenge us because they care more about our growth than their comfort
- rely less on performing and entertaining, and are poised to interrupt things that don't work in order to present things that will
- provide the feel of a conversation or dialogue rather than a one-way broadcast, talking *with* you and not *at* you

There's something special about communicators who have a heart to serve us. Take Jimmy Fallon, for example, who is among the most endearing talk-show hosts we've ever had on air. He values the audience he serves, he's clear about what he's committed to cause, and he knows who he will be in the process. As a result, his gift is always present at every show whether he is spot-on or not.

Speak with an intention to serve others today and watch how they respond.

32. Never compromise when you apologize. Anything less than a full apology is manipulation.

Unless you're perfect (*too late*), the need to apologize is perpetual in your work life. From broken commitments, unmet expectations, betrayals, or hurtful words down to slight oversights and things that may be considered insignificant, we fall short. We are *not* perfect. Most people are somewhat gracious when it comes to our breakdowns now and then, because they know theirs is coming soon to a situation near them. But what is not tolerable and adds insult to injury is when we don't handle apologies with the care and seriousness they deserve. There is a right way to reconcile with others—one that honors the other person to the point where the matter truly ends up as water under the bridge. In contrast, there are ways of apologizing that make the water and the tension rise—only to have the dam break at some point in the future and cause more catastrophic damage.

> The closest we'll ever get to perfect is not found in the absence of breakdowns, but how we handle them when they occur.

Apology 101: When you cause grief in someone's life, don't just throw out a flippant "I'm sorry." *Sorry* can be said with such disdain and manipulation that it warrants more potent language—language you'll have to get grounded in, like, "Would you forgive me?" As you know, "I'm sorry" can be dispensed with no emotion or serious-ness, while asking for forgiveness sets the tone that you're intent on reconciliation. An apology is often a one-way communication that can be done casually, even with malice, and doesn't give the other a chance to release the offense for a true clearing. Asking for forgiveness requires that we step into the humility of an authentic appeal and is a two-way exchange in which both parties participate in real reconciliation. Asking for forgiveness brings an authenticity and transparency to the process that improves everything.

Never make light of how you impacted the other person, no matter the magnitude of the breakdown. A person's experience of what transpired is *their* experience, and it's as real as it gets for them. Just because you wouldn't experience something the way they did doesn't invalidate it for them. We are all different, and to put it bluntly, it's both ignorant and arrogant to think the way *we* (as individuals) process hurt or anger is the only way that is valid. Trivializing the breakdown imminently leads to a one-way, dead-end street, and business is tough enough as it is without going down that road.

A way to prepare yourself for apologies that end well (or even create new beginnings) is to take an honest look at what the offense would be like if you were its victim. Live there for a moment and you'll see in short order that it would have been no fun to be on the other side of *you* in that moment. A little empathy goes a long way.

> An apology with a sad excuse attached to it is a sad excuse for an apology.

To avoid future breakdowns of a similar kind, know that curiosity is not conflict's best friend. In fact, you can't be angry and curious at the same time: it's physiologically impossible. If your breakdown with someone was a bit obscure or not so overt, somewhere in the reconciliation process ask the other why your offense was so impactful. Get curious about it, and you may learn something new that refines the brand you are becoming. Once you understand the reasoning behind someone's pain, it's easier to shift future behaviors to avoid repeated offenses with them and others. This helps us find those critical blind spots that hurt our brand and can remain hidden, in some cases for decades.

Lastly, check in a day or so after the reconciliation and simply ask something along the lines of, "Are we good? Is there any residue we need to deal with?" This shows you care and reveals any afterthoughts, ultimately driving a nail in the coffin of the breakdown so it doesn't live and breathe again in the relationship.

 You may need to apologize for something; if so, do it with care and dignity today.

33. Going to make a referral? Here's a five-point inspection before making the connection.

Ever receive a referral from someone that goes nowhere fast? No callback? Nothing but crickets? How about ones where you meet, but nothing lands as there's no tangible need, synergy, or even opportunity? What about ones that *do* land, but end in short order due to important information not shared up front? It's pretty frustrating, not to mention a waste of time and energy. Unfortunately, many people view a business referral as a name wave or a quick intro— "Hey, Sarah, meet Bob. Bob does *X* and it would be good for you to meet (I think)."

When it comes to connecting relationships, one thing often forgotten is that we will lose a bit of personal brand equity and credibility every time we facilitate a flawed referral. It's the omission of specificity about basic and obvious details for both parties and their situations that often has the introduced parties saying, "What the heck were you thinking?"

> Reflect before you connect. Inspect for a grade after the connection is made.

Here are five key things to consider when giving a referral:

1. Have you shared the specific nature of your contact's requirements with the referral—important details including things like pricing, timing, expectations, requirements, and so on so they know what they're getting into?

2. Has the referral you're providing been described to your contact with enough detail so your contact can decide if there's a fit *before* the referral is made? Just the basics will do.

3. Do you absolutely know, without question, the one who you are referring is proven and will do a brilliant job? Not knowing is gambling for everyone involved.

4. Have you considered whether both parties will get along and work well together? Personalities and skill levels have a lot to do with whether referrals work out or not.

5. Have you told both parties (in your own way) that you value both relationships and would appreciate it if everyone was treated with courtesy, respect, and professionalism? Although presumptive, I never leave this out.

The quality of every referral is in direct proportion to the depth and level of detail we provide in teeing them up. A name wave is not a referral.

Consider who you're connecting others to today.

34. InCONsistency will always rob your brand.

Notice the word "con" in inconsistency. Now consider how conned you feel when those around you agree to do things and are inconsistent in their delivery. Although the world of business places great value in action, movement, and forward progression, a business's predictions, moves, and momentum are found in consistency more than sporadic or flash-in-the-pan performances. People love it when someone shows up with a great accomplishment now and then, but without consistency, *anyone*, no matter how great a performer, is generally branded a "flake" and is a liability to the company and its efforts.

> Inconsistency doesn't work . . . consistently.

You've heard it and you've said it: "Just tell me what's real. Tell me what you can do and do it, and if you can't, let me know." This is the order of the day in life at work, at home, and everywhere else, and it provides others with three mission-critical gifts: clarity of what's real, peace of mind in what *will* happen, and a greater ability for them to be consistent with their commitments. It's also an accurate reflection of our personal brand reputation and a measured indicator of whether we will be invited into what's next . . . or left behind to struggle in our inconsistency.

Never take chances with your brand; be consistently consistent with consistency today. ☺

101

35. If we need to quickly change our attitude on something, it's best we use our brain for a change.

Although they happen hundreds of times every day, we generally don't give enough consideration to our **thought defaults**—thoughts we immediately have when a difficult or uncertain event, situation, or conversation takes place at work. Defaults live and breathe in our minds and tend to weave themselves into a repetitive pattern that has deep repercussions in every circumstance. They resemble the following: When X happens, I usually or always feel, think, or act this way. The question is, does your pattern enhance your position or weaken and sabotage it? Does your pattern move you to hold a problem as gain or pain? Do you get excited when your workload gets intense or do you feel overwhelmed? Spending time adjusting your defaults is the fastest way to bring the right perspectives to create the best attitude to drive the most productive behaviors.

> When you encounter a wall on your business journey, do you feel fear, or think solution? The "ladder" is better.

Benjamin Zander, teacher and conductor of the Boston Philharmonic, shares the idea that problems or obstacles we create or encounter in life don't need to be instantly debilitating; they can be undeniably fascinating. He goes on to say that opportunities to look at adversity through the lens of curiosity are vast, and that our defaults can reduce the biggest of challenges, whether self-inflicted or brought upon us, regardless of magnitude. When you hold adversity in this light, it creates greater mental capacity to explore rather than deplore, then adjust the default to serve you.

We can choose to be fascinated instead of *exacerbated*. In my first book, *Shift Your Thinking*, I tweak the word to "addversity." I accentuate the word *add*, because there are no books, therapy, seminars, or other tools that can *add* more value than when we choose to see walls as steps and trials as gain. But it does require the default of skepticism or fear to be replaced with optimism and courage.

Pay close attention to your defaults. Be fascinated by challenges today.

36. Presentation preparation is much like parachute preparation: a little work will ensure the outcome doesn't fall flat.

No matter what position you're in, the need to prepare and deliver presentations is inevitable. When the time comes, how you present is a platform for your brand to gain serious traction or fall back a few notches.

If presenting to a company in a sales capacity, a best practice is to always conduct thorough research on the company you're meeting with—and its competitors—before you present, so you can speak the same language and address *what's real* with confidence. You'll build empathy, trust, and relatability, and it makes your brand shine brighter than the next presenter(s). Also, nail down the company's unmet needs in detail and base your entire presentation on meeting those needs. Inquiring in advance on what the client's exact expectations are for the meeting and what they would like to experience is mission critical to a great encounter. If you have more to offer than their stated needs, hold off on presenting the big picture until you address exactly what they brought you in for.

> The ability to present well—to move people to connect, engage, embrace, follow, and advocate—is your brand's biggest asset.

If presenting to individuals (inside your company or outside) it helps to know in advance all attendees who will be in the meeting. LinkedIn, Facebook, Pinterest, and other social channels will help you learn about their personality, business style, hobbies, clubs and associations, mutual contacts, and so on, so you can engage in conversations that go beyond the presentation into building a personal relationship. These are the things that make people truly appreciate you, and people liking you builds a great deal of confidence and ease into your presentation.

Next, get an idea of the room setup before you arrive. Although you can email, I prefer a phone call to inquire about the realities of the room. This will allow you to engage in conversation and get clear as to what you will experience when you arrive. Once, and I do mean one time only, we made the mistake of preparing a comprehensive presentation that we couldn't present because the room configuration wouldn't allow it. Also, ask if you can come in early to set up. Nothing's worse than contending with technology and distributing materials while the attendees are staring, wondering why you didn't ask to come in early in the first place.

Also test-drive your presentations. Conduct a dry run or two. As one of our team members puts it: "Practice, drill, and rehearse," or be mediocre at best. Test runs minimize pre-meeting stress and will get you and your team focused and aligned. They will also allow you time to get grounded on the pace, posture, and feel of the meeting. It's amazing how many unnecessary elements of a presentation will get restructured or discarded for a more focused straightforward presentation when practiced. Presentations are very much like a piece of machinery: any unnecessary parts added in will break down the machine. It also helps to be cognizant of the questions that might be asked and prepare great answers in advance. Trust me, clients today will know if you prepared and how much. Don't wing it.

To get the room talking right away, review the expectation you received early on, ask for confirmation, then ask if there's anything else they'd like covered in the meeting. This shows a *present* concern, and it will calm your nerves as the goal of your meeting will be clarified. It also puts attendees at ease because they know you'll be addressing their specific needs, not veering off into alternative agendas. You'll be able to focus in on what the room sees as important or relevant. If 80 percent of your presentation directly relates to the core needs, you've done a superior job of presenting. If it's all relevant, you'll generally win the room.

Prepare for the presentation and watch the brilliance present itself today.

37. Why would others want to help, guide, direct, or teach you if you put out a know-it-all vibe?

The funny thing about "knowing it all" is that it's actually true: we know *all that we know*. But with that truth, I couldn't defend a class-action lawsuit. (I could, but I'd lose.) I couldn't fill a cavity (well I could, but repeat business just wouldn't repeat), nor could I fix a fine watch in a timely manner. Candidly, I can barely assemble a fake Christmas tree with instructions and some aspirin.

The tragic thing about holding on to the idea that we know it all (or even know a lot) is that we miss receiving the knowledge of so many around us. So yes, a know-it-all disposition relationally ropes off the potential for others to engage and speak into our lives with the brilliance *they are*—and everyone has brilliance in their own way. As a result, we remain captive to our own knowledge, intake, and experience. This makes our brand value somewhat one-dimensional and, in many cases, limiting to what is possible in the realm of learning and value expansion.

Many years ago, a friend of mine told me about a group called Convene. It was a monthly gathering of groups of twelve to fifteen CEOs that would meet together for an offsite all-day meeting and support each other with their knowledge, feedback, connections, and encouragement. It sounded intriguing to me, but it was a substantial investment of both money and time. Still, I decided to give it a shot.

After about six months of participating in Convene, a few things were apparent. First, the people I thought would know everything . . . *didn't*. The second thing that became clear was that we all were adding serious value to each other, and in many ways needed each other to see things through different lenses. Whatever capital investment

I made in the group was fractional compared to the upside. One of the hidden values I never considered on the front end was that I was learning things I never would have received in life on my own, and I was now able to dispense those insights to others in a counseling, advisory, writing, and speaking capacity. I also joined a smaller five-man accountability group comprised of some A-players to work on my spiritual life, as well as a couples' group with the same level of people to work on my marriage. I have remained in these groups for years, and although I may end up on sabbatical from time to time, I ultimately go back because the value is substantial and an island is a lonely place to be.

> Back in the day, Jerry Levy, a vendor of ours, told my business partner and me, "If you guys put your heads together, you might come up with a good brain." We laughed, and of course . . . agreed. Thanks, Jerry.

There are a few things to consider when joining or forming groups. You'll want to find people who are aligned to a well-spelled-out objective. It helps to find people from your industry with a diverse array of expertise so they are complementary to one another, not redundant. Or if it's a group to perfect a particular craft, a similarity of skill sets is obviously an asset. Also consider the character of those coming to the table. You want people who are committed to the process and will show up, stay focused, and give 100 percent to the process and relationships, inside and outside the group.

When you assemble for the specific purposes of feedback and knowledge development, you brand yourself as open, curious, and teachable: one who is willing to listen closely, receive the feedback, and (most critically) act on what is shared. Frankly, it is an insult to other people when they take the risk to give their gift of knowledge, and we agree with it but don't act on what we learn.

Consider aggregating many great heads to gain a genius brain today.

38. No severity of inhale can take back a single word spoken.

Our work life is comprised of words: words on the phone, words by a coffee machine, words in passing, words in a meeting, words in conflict. Words, words, and more words—some that we're glad we said and others we wish we could inhale. The things we say can be conduits to a better brand both professionally and relationally at work. But equal, or more important, are the things that we *don't* say.

> Sometimes we speak at a pace too fast, and our insights and wisdom trail a few thoughts behind our words. It's called the pace of stupidity.

Years ago, my wife said something that forever changed my life for the better (other than "I do"): "Dean, I've seen and received enough feedback from others to know that you make a real difference with people. You have a way of seeing things and sharing things that changes people's circumstances and improves their lives. But I believe you'd be even more effective if you exercised more restraint." I instantly knew what she meant, and said, "Tell me more about that." She went on to share that whenever she saw me address a circumstance quickly, my effectiveness percentage was about 70 percent, but on occasion, I'd "miss it" completely. I didn't enjoy those times; in fact, no one did. But she also said that whenever she saw me showing restraint, patiently waiting and allowing the conversation to unfold rather than ripping it open and stepping in too soon, that I would rarely miss and it was received better because my heart was in the right place when I spoke.

We've all experienced times when silence seemed a bit uncomfortable and there was an undue pressure to fill the space with words. I've been there a million times myself and will certainly be there again. But there is great opportunity to restrain and speak at the pace of wisdom and awareness in what is going on while allowing those around you to bring their voice to the table. I've noticed since I've exercised more restraint that there are more opportunities for others to bring their wisdom to the table because my mouth is shut, giving a chance for theirs to be open. In a team environment this is especially critical, because there can be tendencies at times for us to be a polarizing factor, and miss leveraging the full wisdom available from the room.

> Hurtful words are like a razor-sharp
> boomerang. Catch my drift?

Of course in conflict, restraint takes on a whole new meaning. When we're angry, insight and sensitivity to relationship trail miles behind our words, and in the time it takes to sneeze, we can verbally burn a bridge that we may have needed to cross at some point in the future. Let's face it: there are times we want to verbally assault a person just for sport, thinking that somehow the anger is going to magically translate into progress. But most of the time it translates into *regress*, putting you further behind than you were when the conflict started. Not good for a relationship, not good for business, and certainly not good for your brand.

Self-control is a gift we give to others even when they don't deserve it. But more than that, it's a gift we give to ourselves whereby each exercise of self-control or restraint strengthens us into a more resilient, resolved person who becomes virtually bulletproof from the day-to-day offenses or attacks that come our way.

**◄ Practice restraint and self-control with your ►
words and see what *doesn't* happen today.**

39. There are four different personality styles with thirty-two configurations. Are you saying things the wrong way to the right person?

Now that we've discussed restraint in communication, let's discuss the appropriation of communication. This is one of the most powerful tools you'll ever learn to become more effective with your words.

About twenty years ago I literally stumbled across a class called something like "Saying the Right Thing to the Right Person, a Journey into Personality Styles and Why They Matter." I wasn't signed up for the course but asked the woman out front if there were any spaces left; surprisingly, she allowed me to go in without paying. Little did I know it would be one of the most career-impacting seminars of my life. I learned that in all the things we say, no matter how brilliantly they are said or how compelling we deem them to be, our words will be devoid of value and facilitate results that are far from what we want if we are not saying them in a way that will *resonate* with the kind of person we are speaking to. I began to think about where I was in my career, my closing percentages in sales, what success I was having with people buying into my strategy and creative solutions and thought, *Hey, time to start experimenting.*

> We must own our words, embrace their power, see value in their refinement and put the fullness of who we are into each of them. In many ways, we are our words.

As my company grew larger and the accounts got bigger, there were more people in the room at every pitch or presentation than ever before. More personality styles, more backgrounds, more experiences, more biases—but little did they know I was armed with wisdom from that personality class I had taken. In my first (post-class) pitch there were several people in the room including the CEO (the "what's-the-bottom-line" *controlling* personality), the CFO (the "what's-the-ROI, why-should-I-spend-money-on-this" *analytical* personality), the VP of sales and marketing (the "how-will-this-make-me-a-hero-and-make-my-job-easier" *promoting* personality), and the VP of operations (the "what's-it-going-to-take-to-make-all-this-happen, what-will-I-have-to-do" *supportive* personality). Each person in the room had a completely common goal—to build the company—but each of them had individual motives and needs, and they wanted to have an individual understanding of why this was important and why we were the right choice. *So off I went.*

What I noticed first (without thinking about it) was that I was addressing each person in the room as an individual, where before I was addressing the room as a whole in more of a broadcast form. There was a relational connection to each person that I'd never felt before and a relatability that was natural—not forced or contrived. Heads were nodding, minds were melding, and they were grateful I could relate to each person's reality and what each person wanted to have happen. What was once a broadcast became a series of intimate conversations that engaged the audience to interact and take ownership of what was being shared. I had no idea it was going to be that way, and it ended up being the best presentation I'd ever given.

Beyond that, it was rewarding as I brought hope to individuals—not just the company—built trust, and valued everyone in the room. I told the CEO the bottom line of what was going to happen if they used our agency; I told the CFO that they would never spend more money than we would make for the company; I told the vice president of sales and marketing how much more effective and efficient their marketing and their job would be; and I shared with the VP of operations that the brand of the company would be improved and enhanced so they'd have more resources to do more things and buy more equipment. It was a laser-like delivery system of relevance for each person in the room. The result? My closing percentages increased, and my relatability, likability, and sales ability improved miraculously. My brand went from being a "good pitch guy" to a "guy they wanted to do business with" (even liked)—and I'd take the latter any day of the week.

> Communication without consideration is a vague articulation without resonation that ends up as aggravation.

Beyond sales presentations, there are the day-to-day work interactions in which we are not pitching but explaining, conversing, delegating, reprimanding, justifying, conveying, encouraging, and all other forms of speech. The same principle holds true here. The more strategic you are about the way that you deliver things, and the more attuned you are to who it is you are speaking to, the more progress you will make and the more rewarding your relationships will be.

Although I recommend it, you may not choose to get schooled in the art and science of personality styles and the ways to communicate with each. But even if you don't, there's a simple and easy way to get to know how others like to be communicated to, *and that is to humbly ask.* Generally, we sense when we're not communicating well and aren't getting through to others. Simply sharing with them that we acknowledge we may not be connecting well and asking them how we might best communicate will do three things: it will show that we care, it will reveal much about our commitment to the relationship, and it will make communication more effective in the future.

If by chance you don't feel comfortable enough with certain people or certain circumstances to ask for feedback on how you're communicating, a simple look at what happens after you communicate will say a lot about what you're saying and how it is landing. What do their facial expressions say? Does your communication spur further inspiration and dialogue, or does the conversation fall flat, somewhat silent, and generate blank stares? Do you find others looking for a way to segue from what was just said? There are many signs to look for, and we should embrace what we see, as it will refine what we say.

Great personal brands will never take the victim stance and say, "They didn't listen to me." What they will say is, "Perhaps I failed to communicate in a way that worked," and even more courageously, they may perhaps admit they need to learn how to communicate better. Communication is an immediately changeable asset. If we've been communicating in a certain style (without detailed consideration), we can be much more aware and strategic about how we communicate as a gift to those we work with from now on.

Consider who you're talking to and think about how you can more effectively resonate with them today.

40. "Everyone wins" is not a reality we will always be able to create, but it's a commitment that will win everyone over.

This isn't one of those everybody-gets-a-trophy, there-are-no-losers, milquetoast, or politically correct points of view about everyone winning. That's just not how life works, and I would never promote that as anything but an unfounded delusion. Life and all its ups and downs has a way of grinding maturity and strength into us via *not* winning, so there's value there too. But there is a different point of view on "everyone wins" that's worth exploring in the professional environment, as it should be one of the core tenets of anyone's personal commitment at work.

> One of my favorite questions to ask someone facing a challenge or setting a goal is, "So what does a win look like for you?" Then I get to help them get there.

Several years ago, I worked with an Inc. 500 fastest-growing company to create their brand, starting with their mission, vision, and core values. It was an innovator company doing great things in their space, and they were getting a reputation as a go-to place to work. The CEO was pretty unconventional, as indicated by the mock Godfather painting of him in the lobby smoking a cigar. We didn't know whether we were going to get a new client or get whacked by the time we left our first meeting, but we hit it off well and he wasn't as violent as assumed.

When we presented the mission, vision, and core values, I started the mission conversation off by sharing some things I'd heard about how he helped people in his business life. I reminded him of a comment he once made that everyone in the company was a stakeholder in the company's growth and success. I also shared how important he felt it was that his candidates, partners, and vendor alliances also shared in the success of the company and were treated with respect and appreciation beyond the norm. I finished the tee-up with how he shared that even the UPS and FedEx drivers were no different than an employee or vendor. So I hit the presentation slide, and the mission was set in two words: Everyone Wins. He smiled, and I went on to say that *mission* is about what we wake up in the morning and get out of bed to do at work. It's what we stand for, and the idea that "everyone wins" can take place not just in the work environment but everywhere in life—making it a mission worth living for a future worth having.

Make sure everyone wins today.

41. *Truth* is never concerned with what *lies* ahead.

Every day in corporate America people are dishing out everything from subtle departures from the truth to out-and-out lies to cover their tracks, make themselves look good, stay in control, shift the blame, and more. However, the liabilities that exist in less-than-truthful communication of any kind are substantial: a single lie can knock us down the ladder a few rungs or have us gathering our belongings in a cardboard box at the end of the day. Lies, in many ways, are like cholesterol to the heart. A little indulgence here and there doesn't seem like a big thing—until it adds up to deadbeat status.

> Great brands deliver the truth, the whole truth, and nothing but the truth.

When someone considers employment at a company, one of the drivers of their decision has to do with whether they can trust the people they work with. Money, perks, reputation, and so many other considerations pale in comparison to the value of having a trusting relationship with others. And if trust is absent (or even suspected to be absent), people will run, not just walk, from an enticing opportunity. Trust is one of those attributes that is highly prized in corporate culture. For obvious reasons, when we work for a company we have a natural instinct to be "deep in the trenches" with our comrades, fighting it out daily with the inherent challenges of business as well as other realities that make us hope that trust is present and we can count on the team.

But there is accountability here, inside and out. The moment someone contaminates the workplace by lying is really the beginning of the end of their tenure there. The reason for that goes beyond getting caught and fired. Derivations from the truth and flat-out lies slowly poison our brand and stop the satisfaction that can come from it. And although lies, concealments, and exaggerations may have an impact on our colleagues, teams, and successes at work, they do far more damage to our spirit, confidence, and mindset. They cast a shadow that can have others saying to themselves, "I'm just not sure I can trust them" and us saying to ourselves, "This is not who I really want to be." It's a certain lose-lose proposition.

I know this from experience, because as a young twentysomething sales executive, I used to "round things off to the nearest exaggeration." If I was on a sales pitch and was sharing about my company and discussing employee count, I would share I had thirty employees when I only had twenty-six. If we were doing 8.7 million a year in revenue I would tell people we were at 10 million in revenue. If we brought a company to a top 18 position in their category through our marketing efforts, I would round it off to the top 10. Because I feared not being adequate, I never felt comfortable delivering the absolute truth and accepting the repercussions it would have, and I never felt comfortable in my own skin. I didn't trust that the truth would do its job, yet I was hurting myself more than anyone else and not giving myself the gift of living in truth and clarity. The moment I started to share things exactly the way they were was one of the more freeing moments of my life.

> Deviation from the truth awakens the skeptic in our spirit and the detective in our mind.

I doubt many readers are out-and-out liars, but it's the *situational adjustments to our truth* that will hurt our reputation and subvert our fulfillment at work and life. Whether slighting a number, not sharing the fullness of our convictions, or covering up a breakdown, the sum total of these departures from truth will do nothing more than add to our subtraction, multiply our stresses, and divide relationships.

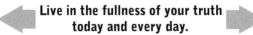

Live in the fullness of your truth today and every day.

42. The quickest way to get a good name in your company is to remember the names from the company you're in.

There are many ways we can improve our brand within our work spheres, in our marketplaces, and in social situations. But if there was one single practice that could have a more immediate and positive effect on our brand (especially in new relationships) it would be remembering people's names.

I'm not certain why it is, but people are astonished when we remember their names and hold us in high regard when we do so. In my book *Shift Your Thinking*, I address this issue, and I'm covering it here because I couldn't write a book that focused on our brand at work without it. There are so many emotional, relational, and even financial advantages that exist in remembering names that it demanded a revisit and expansion. To this day, I always add a few brand points onto someone I've just met when they use my name, or perhaps introduce me to someone they know using my name, or depart while saying, "Nice to have met you, Dean." My first instinct is not to credit these people for being skilled at name retention. Instead, I am grateful and impressed that they cared enough and were present enough with me to remember and use my name.

Most people I discuss the subject with tell me they are "not good with names," but that excuse just doesn't hold water. It's an auto-response that flies out of the mouth because the truth would be too uncomfortable to say. And the truth is along the lines of, "I'm sorry, I don't care enough about you, nor did I put much effort in to remember your name."

When someone tells me they're not good with names, I'll say, "Consider that you're as good as you choose to be, and depending on what is at stake, you are quite good." I go on to ask them, "If there were one million dollars on the line, post-tax, in a duffle bag and all you had to do to receive it is remember the name of the person you were just introduced to, would you succeed?" The answer is always a resounding, "Yes!" They'd say, "I'd repeat it, write it down, put it in my phone, tattoo it on my arm, whatever it took, I would remember their name." The truth is that somewhere between "it doesn't matter very much" and "one million dollars," our priority and capacity to remember someone's name is clearly revealed.

> People who care little about others are
> people who others care little about.

As with all habits and disciplines, this skill takes focus, practice, effort, and measurement to refine. However, at the core of this discipline is *caring*, and somehow caring goes a long way for improved retention—you can go from a D+ to maybe a B- simply by choosing to care about it. Put in a little extra effort beyond caring and you'll become a solid B, and that's better than 95 percent of all mankind.

Knowing we will forget the names of others on occasion, what are some of the social graces and tools that can be used to improve the name game? If you say, "Nice to meet you, Sarah," when you're with someone you just met, and for some reason their name disappears into the abyss within a few minutes, one easy solution is to simply ask: "I'm sorry, I forgot your name. What is it again?" By the second time you'll reconnect to what you heard the first time and have a better chance to remember. Sometimes, if someone has shared a unique name and I can't remember it, I'll simply ask them, "By the way, how do you spell your name?" (Incidentally, this doesn't work well with names like Bob, Mike, or Beth.) As for tools, I find my mobile phone and a basic notes app to be a great way to log, categorize, and access people's names that you'll remember because you cared enough to have a system to do so.

 Google "remembering people's names" and learn more on the subject today.

43. Your professional life is nothing more than "up until now and from now on." Up until now it's been one way, and from now on it can be something entirely different.

One of my biggest joys in life is convincing someone that things can change instantly. It may not always seem that way, and some will argue that change of any real substance takes time. But after asking them to consider that the view of the "long process of change" they are arguing for is being kept alive by their defense of it, I'll suggest that taking a stand that change can happen immediately might begin to serve them well. Rethinking the seemingly impossible may just reshape a tired, useless paradigm while ushering in a more disciplined thought life and extraordinary potential.

> The wall of pessimism spreads to infinity in both directions.
> A perspective of optimism makes that wall one inch high.

It's a little-known fact that the word *discipline* (which we all know is necessary for success) comes from a Greek military term. It means to take the branch of a tree, strip away all that's unnecessary so you can sharpen the branch into a spear, and go to battle. Discipline in this context means to *remove* the things that don't work to make way for optimum function.

The battle that takes place in our mind is no different. It requires we rid ourselves of a thought life that doesn't work to make way for a thought life that breeds brilliant thoughts. I use the word *breed* because one brilliant thought has the capacity to produce more, just like a negative thought has the capacity to multiply and compound. The full impact of this is made more evident if looked at scientifically. People who think with continual negativity over their lifetime can develop a physical "caving in," if you will. Postures will hunch, shoulders round in or drop, facial expressions will form to a frown or a sad look. Even some internal ailments, chronic conditions, and diseases can be caused by the pressure and stress associated with unmanaged thinking that migrates to the negative. Thought is powerful in that it can build and expand you or reduce and limit you, depending on how you govern its direction and momentum.

I once sat with a young man who went into great detail about a challenge he was having with a problem client. He finished his rant with, "They're ruining my life." After I let him get it all out, I simply said, "Yeah, perhaps they have been ruining it . . . up until now." He looked puzzled and asked what I meant. I said, "Everything you told me exists in the 'up until now.' Let's spend a few moments in the 'from now on.' Let's see what's possible there." He was so locked in to the "up until now" he couldn't even explore what was possible in the "from now on." As soon as he stepped into a from-now-on mindset, possibilities opened up, and I didn't even need to advise him on next steps. He did that himself and left the up until now behind.

> The grace of change is that it is timeless. It can happen at anytime, anywhere, anyplace.

The cornerstone to facilitate rapid change is acknowledging that our belief system can be adjusted in just a few seconds to a few minutes. It can happen as quickly as a decision, and it will bring us to an immediate and notable transformation in communication, behavior, and result.

But the real value of the "up until now and from now on" principle is found in its availability. Like a heartbeat, it's always working in the present moment. Right now or in five minutes or one hour from now, "from now on" will be available. Tomorrow at 2:13 PM it will be there, and in fact it's open for business 24/7 and accessed by a simple realization. That's the opportunity associated with change when you hold your life and work as nothing more than "up until now it's been one way" and "from now on will be different."

The words "fresh start" never get stale, and living in the "from now on" reflects well on your brand and serves as an inspiration to others.

Move boldly and confidently into the "from now on" today.

44. If you are not learning at a pace quicker than things are changing, your brand will lack relevance.

As a mentor to professionals at all levels, I've made a pretty surprising discovery: 95 percent of the people I meet with do not have a specific plan in place to become a thought leader in their area of business. Generally, when I ask them how much time and effort they put in on a weekly basis to learn more about their field, their position, industry trends, and new discoveries, the answers inevitably come back as "a little," "not much," or "not at all." They go on to justify the answer by saying that they are learning on the job, which is not a bad thing, it's just a given . . . and not much credit should be awarded for what's expected—especially for those who want to excel in their careers.

Learning at the pace of osmosis will have us growing at the pace of osmosis in our business, plus we'll never be able to bring more new contributions to the table than what others would be able to bring, so we'll just blend in to the status quo. What enables us to be a standout brand within our company? Someone who is recognized and moved into better positions over time must be one who is bringing to the table consistent new growth ideas, preventative measures, problem-solving strategies, current industry realities, case studies, and more.

> It's hard work getting in the circle of "who's who." Once there, you better make certain you're up to speed on "what's what."

I can tell you with near certainty you can move from a basic position of knowledge to being well under way as a thought leader in your workplace via a consistent commitment to learning. Currently, thought leaders spend about five hours a week learning the various aspects of the business they're in and all that surrounds it. And today there are so many avenues to get specific information about your area of business that all excuses for not expanding your knowledge base are gone. Before internet searchability, information was accessible, but you had to go to great lengths to get it. Today, with the stroke of a key and some creative word and phrase searching you'll be able to pick up content online that will accelerate your learning and improve your value to others. You have access to books, audio files, videos, articles, blogs, and random rogue bits from practitioners to experts to thought leaders and everyone in between. The good thing about this research is that you can subscribe to many of these information sources to create an ongoing stream of focused information. But be discerning here, as bad information absorbed is bad information dispensed.

> Things move so fast today that by the time we acquire knowledge, it's outdated. New information is key to real progress these days.

Having the discipline of learning consistently builds a sustainable confidence and self-assurance that fine-tunes our attitude, our communication, and our presence while adding to the *joy at work* factor we hear about but so seldom experience. In short, the amazing way learning makes us feel and the courage it gives us is worth whatever price we'd pay to turn off the TV or get up a little earlier to do some critical learning. The great news is when we begin a journey of learning about our job, our company, and our industry, added confidence starts immediately—as well the impact that you will have on your company and the people in it.

Develop a path to becoming a thought leader in your work today.

45. You generally don't have to walk a mile in someone's shoes to get the feel of what others are experiencing. Usually a few steps will do just fine.

They say in business that it's what we don't know that can hurt us. True, but in relationships, it's what we don't know about others that *disconnects us.*

Case in point: One of the executives I used to work with was a very difficult personality to be with when there was a problem of any kind. As CEO, every time I tried to course-correct what he was doing, there would be such a pushback that I almost gave up on him—that is, *fired him.* In talking with a mutual friend, I shared this situation so I could get some honest feedback on how best to navigate the relationship, and I inquired if he knew why there was always such pushback in correction. He shared with me some background on the executive's past that helped me understand areas of work where the executive was apt to be more vulnerable now when corrected. So I adjusted my approach in communication with him. It changed everything for us. Performance was improved and the stress level (as we grew) was tolerable.

> Relational insightfulness doesn't necessarily need to be a gift that we possess; it can be found in the due diligence we undertake.

Aside from the benefit of doing a little due diligence on people to help solve problems, you'll also know some details of their background that will help you to have a better relationship. With a little online digging via social channels, you'll generally find relational gold in the form of common interests, passions, or something intriguing or fascinating. Even the process of investigation creates a connection that emphasizes that this person is not just part of a big machine; they have a life, relationships, challenges, passions, hobbies, things they contribute to, and more. It takes them from being somewhat abstract or a number, to being more human—all with a simple glance into their life. Another way to get to know people better is to invite them to lunch or coffee and engage in a get-to-know-you conversation that is focused more on learning about them than broadcasting about ourselves. People appreciate it when we take interest in them, and once a relationship is moved to a new level of quality it generally doesn't return to the original state. You can never have enough quality relationships in the workplace, as they will deliver value back to you at the most obvious or critical times simply because you devoted a bit of effort to them.

When we stay stuck in one place working with people, but choose not to get to know them (which we can do for years), our relationships remain one-dimensional. In contrast, I've seen the value of those who choose to get to know their co-workers and team members at a deeper level. There is a specialness of those relationships that is almost enviable. A little investment goes a long way in this endeavor.

Get to know one of your colleagues at a deeper level today.

46. Successful professionals don't allow one area of their life to spike while the others become a train wreck.

Over the years, I've watched many video interviews of accomplished business people giving accounts of their career progress, goals reached, and lessons learned. They seem to breeze along, sharing at a confident pace about all that transpired in their careers. But without fail, there is always a point in these interviews where either a question is asked about family or they just start talking about family, and the mood changes from confidence and pride to a deep reflection—and in most cases, some *regret*. In just about every case, the individual will talk about broken marriages, kids that are estranged or got into serious trouble, or an immediate family that's busted apart in some way. Often these superachievers will tear up or even cry over the relational carnage that occurred under their watch while they were busy climbing the corporate ladder or building a company. It's like the interview just sobers right up and gets really honest, and for some reason that becomes the most memorable part of the interview.

> Regret becomes the default because we haven't learned from the experience. Growing from the experience minimizes or eliminates the regret.

But family, although critically important to life success, is just one area of a businessperson's life. There are others to consider as well, including one's faith, fitness or overall health, social relationships, passions, and hobbies—all of which are vital to a healthy work-life balance. If all these areas were a bar chart and you were to view them as they relate to a successful life, you'd notice they were all growing consistently; you wouldn't see any one section growing like a weed, while the others were struggling to rise. Generally, when one area or bar is spiking, the other bars are not just halted, they're actually falling, and in some cases, off the chart completely. For example, you might have a workaholic type who makes millions of dollars but ignores their health, only to suffer a massive heart attack and never have a chance to enjoy what was built.

The combinations of potential breakdowns caused by ignoring various bars on the chart of our life are endless, and it would be best to subscribe to having a foundation that raises all bars equally; that will put your life on as solid ground as it will ever be. Everything else will, as they say, make you feel like your feet are firmly planted five feet off the ground—discontented, out of balance, and soon to fall.

The "all things growing at the same rate" discipline is where true success lives. There's a peace that comes from being able to look at all areas of your life at one time and be inspired instead of overwhelmed. It requires you to become comfortable with everything growing a bit slower because you're paying attention to the balance, but life—in all its waking hours and in the soundness of sleep—will be more fulfilling and rewarding, and rarely will something fall into ruin.

The process of bringing strategy, context, and implementation to a good work-life balance begins by evaluating the various areas of your life and doing a deep dig on how well each is performing. This evaluation is typically broken up into two parts. The first is a self-assessment—kind of a "lock yourself in a room" exercise where you think through the various areas in your life and what you and others are experiencing, what's working, what's not, and so on. The next step is to go to the people in your life who are reflected by the various bars of your chart and ask them how you and they are doing based on your performance in those areas. Discovery is the first step, and as mentioned earlier in this book, creating the environment for you and others to be completely honest is going to give you insights into which chart bars need some immediate attention and which ones are working well.

 Check the balance in your life and see how the categories are growing today.

47. Sending an email to someone in the midst of a work conflict usually turns the "e" in email to an e-mbarrassing, e-mpty, e-ruptive, e-nraged, e-rratic, e-nflamed, e-vil, e-xasperating, e-stranged, e-gotistical or e-xplosive mail.

Ever craft an email in the heat of a conflict, hit the send button, and before you count to three, a bit of regret and stress set in—and perhaps a pretty certain feeling that something's going to hit the fan? Then it hits you: "Oh crap, it's in writing and I can't adjust, take back, or hit 'undo.' It's delivered."

I've done this more than I care to admit, and as a twenty-five-year veteran advertising writer who can craft a pretty decent email devoid of emotional inflammation, cuts, jabs, etc., I decided whenever there was a breakdown in a working situation, I was going to forgo the creative written assault and opt for a meeting or a phone call to discuss it head-on. Something told me I was never going to be a master of reconciliation or transformation via email, and I would rather work on my relational skills face-to-face or voice-to-voice.

> That moment in conflict—the one that sets off the horrible—is the moment to consider sharing not manipulating, relating not emoting, giving not taking, accounting not blaming, and empathizing not judging.

When writing an email relating to a conflict or to make a point, it doesn't matter how well you craft it. It is subject to interpretation on the other end, and when emotions are heightened, interpretation goes into overdrive. The results are generally poor and cause more work and stress than necessary. Although email is an amazing tool for fast, efficient, and effective communication to others, it's also very dangerous and subject to massive interpretation when used in heated situations.

On this very day, relationships will end as a result of toxic or misinterpreted emails. Today, someone (or perhaps dozens of people) will get fired as a result of an inflammatory email. Today, lots of bad things will happen as a result of a one-way communication in writing; instead, much better things could happen via a mature, two-way conversational exchange in which you can hear and/or see the other person and respond to the exchange.

Consider stretching your conversational skills in problem solving with face-to-face or voice-to-voice interactions rather than sending a risky email today.

48. We create goals as part of our plans to succeed in life. But what about creating a plan for our goals so *they* succeed?

I think if people were honest about the percentage of goals they set that eventually went nowhere, they'd come up with a high number. I would. The main reason goals are not achieved is there's rarely a specific, workable plan created for the goal itself. Goals typically start off with a lot of excitement, enthusiasm, and an overabundance of optimistic emotions. This, of course, is all prior to starting the goal. Then the inevitable happens: hard work sets in, challenges arise, and feelings change drastically. With no set plan in place and often no clear next steps or thinking given to what will happen when the hard work kicks your motivation to the curb, the goal drifts into obscurity, motivation slams into a rut, and feelings of confidence disappear into who knows where—only to find us later setting a different goal and hitting repeat. It's unfortunate but true that a buildup of unaccomplished goals will actually ingrain itself into our mindset and drape over our attitude to the point where the idea of setting *any goal* seems hopeless, or even ridiculous.

I'll be the first to tell you that motivation is a viable tool in the world of goal achievement, but a good goal plan, along with a solid commitment, is what will keep your motivation durable enough to get to the end of the goal. Some of the preliminary assets within a goal plan are obviously the details, timelines, resources, and tools needed, as well as people you'll need to have access to along the way. And although it's not talked about much, you're going to have to have the physical stamina, emotional wherewithal, and mental strength to endure the journey. This may require adjustments in diet, time for exercise, and perhaps relaxation disciplines, because achieving goals is not an easy endeavor; that's the reason so many goals vaporize.

The process I use is something that I instituted at my branding agency with prospects who were reluctant to sign a big proposal without a test drive of our work. Clients who wanted to take baby steps were not offensive to us; in fact, we were empathetic to their position and figured out a way to kick things off, gain momentum, and start building a successful long-term, loyal relationship. The process was baked in four steps:

1. **Start small.**
2. **Phase in quick wins.**
3. **Measure as you go.**
4. **Build for scalability.**

> Our dreams and visions without strategy and tenacity
> are soon to become nightmares and illusions.

So let's say you have a goal. Knowing that you will need a reference point, start a written document that outlines these four steps:

Start small. Starting with small steps is important because the nature of goals has people wanting to achieve them in one "big bite." In reality, bringing a big goal to completion is just a compilation of planned-out small goals and identified tasks. In fact, I'll always recommend going for a bigger goal if the goal-setter is willing to break that goal into small, achievable steps. The value in starting small is that you will immediately start building successes; small successes create momentum and motivation and keep them breathing. Staring at a really big goal all at once can bring our inspiration to a halt, our perspiration to a flow, and our inclination to continue to a dead stop.

Phasing in quick wins is just what it implies. It's a matter of taking those small, planned-out steps and making sure nothing gets in the way of you accomplishing them within whatever timeline you've set. The value of phasing in quick wins is that it will always course-correct the goal; it will drive you to the places where you need to be and keep you from places where you shouldn't be at a real-world, I'm-getting-it-done pace. Phasing in quick wins has a unique way of identifying the series of *next* quick wins that need to take place for the journey to continue, or even accelerate. Also, these quick wins will provide you with the personal confidence and optimism you need to proceed to the next phase of the goal until it's eventually complete.

> Diligently working on a goal isn't about what it gets you as much as how the work transforms you.

The *measure as you go* step is a discipline of consistent evaluation in the process of what is working and what is not. I've always believed that success is measuring the thing you're working on, and doing more of what works while eliminating the things that don't. That seems simple, and it is, but the only way to measure effectively is to build "checkpoints" into the plan so you can determine what is productive and what is not, who is performing and who is not, what you'll need and what you won't, and so on. This principle has held true in my marketing world; the best possible use of time, money, and resources was to drill down and focus on the few things that we were getting the best results on, working like crazy on those productive items.

Building for scalability is more an outcome of doing the first three points well and with consistency. Starting small, phasing in wins, and measuring will position you to scale what you've done. This way you won't have to force growth: it will happen naturally if you're diligent with the first three points. Without the first three in play, growth will become dangerous for you, and potentially for others who work with you or are invested in you, as future trajectory becomes a "best guess" discipline, not one based on actuality. Building on what is real will inspire just about everyone and everything associated with the process. So as you scale, keep integrating small wins and measuring, and watch the goal become clearer, closer, and easier.

◄ **Bring some process to your goals today.** ►

49. How you feel may be an indicator of where you are in life. How you address and govern your feelings determines who you become.

Infants coming into the world don't have much context or background, so they are essentially feeling-driven machines. Whatever they feel like, they do. Logic and rationale do not reign, nor do infants have any sensitivity to what works in life and what doesn't. They just "feel forward."

Feelings are why when little Johnny (age 3) has his tractor stolen by his younger brother, Joey, Johnny feels like cracking Joey in the head with the tractor, and occasionally does. Repercussions set in, which makes little Johnny realize feelings are not all they're cracked up to be. It might be better to figure out a new way to get his toy back instead of being sent to his room without the coveted tractor.

Then Johnny grows up to be a teenager and gets a job. But one day his *feelings* get the best of him and he just doesn't *feel* like going to work, so he doesn't. The phone rings a few hours later, and it's his boss asking him where he is. When Johnny says he just didn't *feel* like coming to work, his boss replies, "Okay, you don't have to . . . ever. I'll send you your check." Then John gets married, but doesn't *feel* like being faithful; gets a corporate job, but doesn't *feel* like being a team player; has kids and *feels* like working rather than going to little Jane's recital; *feels* like eating whatever he wants and gains fifty pounds; *feels* like doing "good enough" but not "great" work at his job. Feelings emote John's life into serious breakdown in just about every area because his *feelings* hold the keys to drive his life and the commitments he's made to himself and to others.

Feelings are overrated. In and of themselves they do nothing, and candidly, they are responsible for a great deal of self-inflicted difficulty and limitation in our lives.

Given that feelings can wreak havoc in our lives with such magnitude, it's interesting how much we identify our feelings as the person we are. The truth is, we are *not* our feelings. Feelings should never be linked with our identity, and the moment we ignore that truth is the moment everything will be based on our emotion and our mood, not our resolve, innovation, or what we create. I'm not sure why it happens, but at points in our life we decide to merge *how we feel* with *who we are*; that starts the roller coaster of life, where the ups and downs are not determined by choice and commitment, but by the unpredictable ways we end up feeling. It's no surprise, of course, that experiences and circumstances make us feel things; it's how we respond to those circumstances and what we turn those emotions into that is the true core of who we are. So our biggest opportunity is to manage our lives through decision, not emotion. This is possible, but it requires relating to feelings as a third party, choosing to embrace or ignore what is being felt.

As you plan to achieve substantial goals in your career (and I know this will sound strange), I'd suggest sitting down in a quiet place and having a serious "come to terms" conversation with your feelings. It's imperative to discover your own quiet place. For some it's a room with a Do Not Disturb sign on the door; for others, the beach; while others prefer the mountains; but having a go-to space is critical to find resolve in this process.

The idea of negotiating with yourself (which, by the way, you do all day long anyway) to prioritize your emotions as less important than your commitments will help you resolve who and what will be in control of the journey ahead: the decided you or your emotions. The ironic thing is that you may *feel* this is silly, *feel* I'm an idiot, and *feel* like throwing this book in the trash. But you could consider choosing to take new ground and decide to be in a new form of control where negative emotions have zero effect on your vision, your purpose, and your goals.

Imagine a life where feelings aren't the determining factor of what happens or doesn't—a life where feelings that would stop or limit you from what you know to be important are simply referred back to that quiet conversation about who is in control. It's a life that is driven by the promises and commitments we make and discounts feelings as the unpredictable liabilities they are.

Take the feelings that impact your progress and put them in their place today.

50. Leadership isn't something you do, it's someone you are.

It's an incorrect thought that to be a leader you need to be in a leadership position, designated with a title, or be running something—a team, department, or division. Nothing could be further from the truth. There are positions, of course, but leadership is a commitment that each person makes from the excellence they operate in, and that commitment is called "leadership by example." It's the most powerful form of leadership there is. I've known people with positions and titles who couldn't lead their way out of a paper bag, not to mention inspire others. People like that tend to place too much emphasis on their title, waving it like a flag to be acknowledged, and it's only a matter of time before they're discovered as posers, not leaders. If someone is leading by example, it's a different story.

> Management hierarchy is something that shows up in an organizational chart, but leadership is something that shows up in an individual's heart.

Leadership by example is one of those rarely talked about traits in a business, but it's not a rarely noticed trait. People see it, respect it, aspire to be like it, and in some cases will imitate it without a word being said or a title being waved. Either way, the value to the organization is substantial. People who quietly lead by example move up in their professions in ways that may appear unnoticeable, but suddenly promotion, acknowledgment, raises, or conversations about a better, brighter future happen. In fact, I've seen more people who lead by example replace people who lead by position because they walk the walk, seeing no value in just talking the talk. They just do.

Be an inspiration to others and lead by example with excellence today.

51. Fear is a great motivator for success, but a vision to serve others is the best motivator.

During the later years of my dad's life, I suggested we meet for lunch on occasion and talk life. The norm was that most times we were together, we were in the midst of family gatherings where fly-by conversations were the standard; consequently, we never experienced dialogues of any real depth.

During one of these one-on-one lunches, he looked up from his fish and chips, paused for a moment, and asked, "Dean, do you have any idea why I became successful in my career?" I replied, "No, Pops, but by the seriousness of your tone, it sounds like you're going to tell me." He went on to share that the real reason was that he was afraid of failure, and his whole career was built on a foundation of fear moments driving choice and action one after the other—hour after hour, day after day, month after month, and year after year—until his company went public. He shared that every move he made, relationship he formed, and plan he made was to protect himself from losing in life. I asked, "Were you successful?" He shared with me that financially, yes, he was. But he missed out on many things because he was focused on potential loss, and just about everyone in his path of business became a means to get to success. In many ways people became mechanisms, and although my father was respected for his abilities to get things done, I knew in his heart that there was regret about how he went about building his career.

Ironically, his fear never stopped: it just morphed from the fear of losing in business to the fear of relationships not working to the fear of life consequences and so on. Yet I couldn't deny two things: one was that the method my father utilized to build his career *actually worked* to help him become financially successful, and second, the apple (me) didn't fall too far from the tree. A quick look in the mirror revealed that much of my early years in my career were spent in fear mode until I was made aware that there was a bigger game for overall life success and a different motivator to drive it. And that was the motivation to serve others with excellence.

> The clearer your vision to serve others, the more blurred your fears will be when with them.

After a few years of serving forward instead of fearing forward, I remember going into a meeting with a young woman who stopped me in the hallway and expressed a bit of nervousness about it. I told her I could relate and shared that there are two postures to have going into a meeting. One is to focus on oneself, where looking good, being in control, getting what we want, and being all about us is the agenda. Second is the idea of releasing all expectations, forgetting about what we want to get, and focusing our gifts and abilities on serving the people we're meeting with whether we get anything or not. She laughed and said the nerves disappeared immediately, and we had a successful, *relaxed* meeting.

> Nervousness is not a reason to freak out. It's a call to focus in . . . on others.

Fear is a natural part of our life, but when it appears, it's a call to hold things in a different light so the fear takes a neutral position, having no impact on our mental bandwidth or our capacity to serve. Therein lies the shift: to put our focus on giving instead of taking. A posture of taking will always have our eyes on what might be missing, what we won't get, or what might go wrong. A posture of giving puts our focus on what we can provide and what difference we can make. Our eyes are taken off self so there's nothing negative to see, only possibility to look forward to.

Focus on serving others, forget about self, and experience a new day today.

P.S. This has nothing to do with the context of this book, but the brand of me is always looking to make a difference where I can, and I don't want to underplay the value of those last conversations with my father. At the time of writing this book it had only been a year since his death, and it turns out that those conversations are the ones I remember most. I loved my dad, respected him, and was grateful for the life we had, especially those lunches we shared.

Consider your parents, the time you have left, and how you can serve into those relationships— as they are here until they are not.

52. A word on digital etiquette—or how our *smart*phones make us look like idiots.

Whenever I think of the word *etiquette* I think of fine linen napkins, elbows off the table, and fork placement—all of which I give zero thought to in a given day. Seems the days of "proper" have been replaced with "Whatever I feel is proper enough for me." I'm good with that to some degree, and the reason is that lack of etiquette— especially in business these days—has little to do with forks or elbows and has been replaced with a form of digital rudeness so pandemic that a simple turn of the head will bring Digital Rudeness Syndrome (DRS) into view. In fact, before twenty-four hours ticks by, you will likely be the victim (or perhaps the perpetrator) of DRS. Following are a few things to consider.

> A smartphone can connect you to everybody and make the person you're with feel like a nobody.

First, we know smartphones are an asset in the workplace and we know why. What we may not be aware of is the liability they are to our brand. What may be seemingly insignificant or standard perceived operating procedure for smartphone usage may be damaging relationships and stifling opportunities. The good news is there are relatively few moving parts here, and it's not rocket science to make sure that our brand stays intact. It's fairly easy to ensure that those in our presence understand we care more about being in the real world with them than in persistently diving into a digital world outside the meeting or conversation. It's the sporadic ins and outs in the conversation that begin to disengage the experience.

Foundational to smartphone civility is owning the following principle: When you disconnect into digital distraction in the presence of an individual or a group, you genuinely care more about your digital activity than you do about the relationships that are before you. Even if the intention is a pure one, what it screams loud and clear to others is that there's something more important out there than there is right here. People feel it, and generally they don't forget it. In fact, there are people I know who have been etched with DRS at such depth that whenever their name comes up, comments about their DRS usually precede anything else said—and it's not pretty. That's *branded*. What's worse is that we feel quite uncomfortable connecting these people to other valuable relationships in fear that their addiction to their smartphone will end up making *us* look not so smart for making the connection.

The next way to combat DRS is to accept that the real-time nature of data delivery into our phones doesn't mean we need to immediately access that information on the fly in all circumstances and at all times. This is the disease that most seem to live in: "I can't wait fifteen, thirty, sixty, or ninety minutes" to look at something that may be spam or whatever. "But what if it's an emergency?" people say. If it's an emergency, they'll keep calling back, and people understand the need to pick up a constant repetitive call or text combination. And we all know the truth—the chances of it being an emergency are slim to none.

> Great brands control their smartphones instead of their smartphones controlling them.

To eliminate the problem altogether, turn off your phone or put it on vibrate when meeting with others (and put it away). However, if you're expecting an important call, text, or email from someone, simply notify the party or parties you're with that you'll need to address it if and when it occurs. Try to relegate this to one distraction and know that clarifying in advance is the gold standard. People understand these things.

If it's a business meeting and you're going to be utilizing your phone to take notes, notify the individual or the group that you will be doing so in order to not appear rude and/or distracted. Or if there are apps or other such tools needed, again share what is true, so others don't invent what is not.

Consider others when using your technology today.

53. At least once a week, do something so amazing you'll be able to tell a story about it.

Every human being is a book comprised of stories; some stories we experience by happenstance, others we create. Some human books are worth reading. Others are not. That's the clear-cut nature of mankind and why we see some people as interesting—even fascinating—and in contrast view others as beige, nondescript, and well . . . boring. And although I see that all humans have brilliance in them, the world is not always so nice . . . or optimistic.

Some people are dealt the cards of a life full of stories. For instance, there's the army kid who moved to twenty-six countries before she was 18, learned to speak eight languages, and saved her little brother from being eaten by an anaconda in the Amazon jungle—all by happenstance from a life that created countless stories. Others are raised in a small town of 641 people (on a good day), and there was never much in the way of excitement, nor were stories happening except once every year or two. This is not a bad thing, just two different places on the spectrum of living—both that would benefit from the creation of new stories.

> Risk it, then task it. If you don't, you live life in a casket.

So what does it mean to do something at the level that it's worth telling a story about? First off, this is the kind of story we create from nothing, or it's a notable addition onto something that's already happening. It's generally something we've never tried before, or something we believe will have impact, create excitement, and make progress.

145

Usually, it's risk-based, and often the bigger the risk, the better the story, the greater the value. Could be trying something new at work, an experiment—social or actual, going after a big account, or calling a meeting and sharing a big idea. Could be trying a new food or activity, or going to a new place. Could be work related or personal, because this concept has little to do with us going around and telling great stories and more with us *living* great stories—experiencing what they do to us, relishing the value they build into us, and appreciating how others involved in the story get value as well. At the same time, these stories will serve as inspiration for others when shared at just the right time.

Think about what would be story-worthy, and start planning it out today.

54. Efficiency is being organized so you can spend time on what's important, not on what's lost.

My wife thinks I'm a nut. She's right, as usual. But every time something happens in our daily, weekly, or monthly routine that shouldn't happen—things like scheduling issues, dinner and household needs, social mix-ups, and so on—I'll tell her, "We need to make a system or process so that doesn't keep happening." Her response? "Why does everything have to be a system?" I tell her it doesn't, but after I'm done implementing the new process and she sees how much it saves time, saves energy, and eliminates confusion, she still looks at me like I'm from another planet—yet I know she's grateful.

Here's an example of a simple problem—one that is the cause of stress, being late, missing appointments, wasting others' time, and more: misplacing the car keys. Developing an easily accessible location or two to place the keys (and wallet) instead of potentially searching between the couch cushions, in the bathroom, on the shelves, in the pants, in the drawer, or wherever they could land . . . *is a system*. One of my systems is using shower time for creative thinking. Too much information, I know, but bear with me. (Bad choice of words, sorry.) While showering I discovered that most often I would just zone out and drift between thoughts, so I decided to utilize that time differently, and some of my best names, taglines, and other ideas have resulted from this standard daily routine. Traffic time, waiting-in-line time, and (a less appealing reality) even potty time are all opportunities for greater efficiency. Another simple system is to have a go-to list of all the things you need in stores so when you go out to get them, you can save some trips, combine shopping, even buy commodities in bulk to save gas, time, and energy while simplifying your life and having what you need.

> Just about everything you do in your personal and work life can be designed into a process or system that will save time, add capacity, reduce stress, and increase productivity.

In our day-to-day work, creating systems is a requirement for success, especially if the same breakdowns are occurring over and over again. Here are some examples:

- If you want to fix being late to external meetings you need to drive to, a solid system is to view the map and check the "street view" feature online, print full directions, set GPS navigation, and as backup, even call the place you're going and ask if there are any difficulties or things you should know about getting to their location or parking once you're there. Leave early and you'll be more relaxed and focused when you arrive.
- If you want to remember people's names, hobbies, birthdays, and so on, use your smartphone for good: get an app for it, learn the tool, and stay the course.
- If you want to save time, there are many productivity-enhancing apps to help with systems creation, therefore numerous ways to set your life up for total efficiency.
- Going to schedule a meeting? Have a checklist, so you don't miss anything/anyone.
- Going in for a job review? Be prepared with a talking points document outlining the ways you've impacted the business, things you can see improved, things you can improve on, and answers to probable concerns or challenges they may have with you.

> Your brand depends on continuous planned excellence, not dealing with ongoing unplanned circumstances.

It's amazing how much time can go by without really applying much thought to developing systems. Often we're just too busy contending with life to slow down and determine what "better" could look like, figure out what things are causing ongoing grief, or strategize what things we know could be improved on. If by chance you're not process oriented, seek out the help of someone who is. Organized types tend to like to help others become organized. As we reviewed before, this is a great time to *start small, phase in quick wins, measure as you go,* and *build for scalability.* Gaining system momentum is the concept of developing one system and seeing the results, then progressing to the next system and the next until the cogs of routine are moving fast and freely—not clogged up, stuck, and grinding progress to a slow pace.

There's something very inspiring about using the systems you create to enhance your productivity and daily circumstances. With life and business becoming more complex and more competitive, we need all of the time, energy, capacity, and extra strength we can get to compete, grow, and dominate in our space. This is the value that's created when we have a systems mindset. Not to mention, it's a bad reflection of our brand when we have breakdowns in things we do repeatedly and are expected to be good at.

Look at an area in your work or personal life that's not functioning well and develop a system for it today.

55. Your personal brand in business is like building a house of cards: great care goes into its construction, yet with one false move, you'll need to start over.

If you've been reading sequentially, by now you know that building a compelling personal brand isn't for the faint-hearted or partially committed. It takes grit, determination, reaching into your core, and pushing the limits of *you* at work—from the big things down to the small things. And I'm sure you realize that the success of being a great brand goes beyond your work and will make every area of life better in just about every way for everyone you are in relationship with or will soon meet. Work relationships will be stronger; work conditions will be better; family, social acquaintances, and friendships will be better. At the same time, you'll be strengthening your character, creating more opportunity, and gaining more control over your career path and life journey. I'm sure you'll also agree that *not* building yourself into a standout brand might have you on the chopping block of anything you're involved in.

> It's one thing to get your brand to a place and another thing to keep it in that place.

Knowing that your brand is a living, breathing entity, a key area to address is your **brand sustainability**: the ability to maintain your brand and keep it irresistible while moving it to new levels of performance and value. My dad used to say that in order for something to stay in one place, it has to be growing; otherwise, it will be moving slowly backward. This holds true for our personal brand because the nature of all things around us is growing, moving toward progress, pushing to get ahead despite the conditions. The question is, will we be moving along with the growth or watch it pull ahead until it is eventually out of sight and quite possibly out of reach? *This happens every day.*

Using all you've learned in this book so far, along with what you already knew, will be obvious keys to brand sustainability. But there's one area we haven't talked about, and it is one of those subtle bits of wisdom that true business professionals pay close attention to because close attention *needs* to be paid. It's based on a verse in the Bible which talks about *avoiding even the appearance of wrongdoing.* In essence, it means never putting yourself in a position where those around you within either earshot or eyeshot will hear and/or see something that will have them question your brand or your integrity—even if it's not something that would warrant it. It's being conscious there are things you might do, places you might go, people you might hang with, or things you might say that don't seem like they could hurt or fragment your brand, but could have dire consequences. The tough news is, one bad choice, one wrong statement, or one unwise action can make a new reputation spread through the work environment like a flash-fire, and before you know it, you're labeled as the "something" person, whatever the invented "something" happens to be.

> Your brand is not just what you share with others, but what others share about you.

For example, say a guy is interested in getting his wife some lingerie and decides he's going to shop on Victoria's Secret's website on company time. Someone comes around the corner and sees what he's looking at, and there's a quick click off the page with a sheepish look. This is a classic case of the "appearance of wrongdoing"—and there are many. We generally know what these potential brand burners are. Whether it's something we're going to do or something someone asks us to be involved with, we often get this feeling that maybe we shouldn't be doing that. Call it the early-warning brand-detection system. It's a great call to pay attention when those feelings come up.

Heeded, they often keep us in the zone of brand growth and eliminate the "house of cards crash potential" that accompanies these unnecessary things we might do at work.

Just be wise and handle your brand with care today.

56. What failure means and what it means to you. Facilitate Achievement In Life

It's no surprise that when you calculate the total failures of any successful person who's reached significant levels of achievement in their career, the number is substantial. The average number of failures per person is almost comical, and yet they all add up to something amazing. Of course you've heard the story of Thomas Edison, how he had to fail a bazillion times before that lightbulb worked. Well, there are a bazillion more stories just like it, and there will be a bazillion more. Everyone (and I do mean everyone) who's ever become successful will tell you they have their own kind of lightbulb realities along the way, but some will tell you they held failure as having no downside; they held failure with the weight of a feather and gave it no credence other than learning. They moved on, considering the failure(s) as growing forward, not slowing down.

So what stops people from achieving great things, taking great risks, and moving into new territory in their work life? Most often it's the negative thinking and emotion they *attach* to failure. For some reason, society has placed a stigma on failure that puts it in the category of a disease to avoid at all costs. Society as a whole, by the way, is nothing more than a liability of collective confusion: it doesn't have much relevance, doesn't live in your reality, and shouldn't have the credibility to decide anything. *This is up to you.*

> Achieving greatness in business is similar in feel to slipping on a banana peel, but slipping forward!

As a starting point, consider what it might mean to you and your brand to develop a "when failure happens, failure is progress" mindset. Having the right perspectives and approach when failure occurs has the capacity to strip all negative emotions from the experience. Alternatively, it can take you from moving forward with great momentum and optimism and slow you to an emotionally distraught crawl—it can even stop you dead in your tracks.

The difference is in the way we hold failure. Some hold failure so negatively that they position themselves in life to never fail. They end up in that "If you play it safe in life nothing good or bad will ever happen to you, you'll just exist" disposition, and that's no way to live. Others miss the point by holding failure as a form of self-punishment. This means, out of the estimated hundreds of failures they will have during the rest of their business lives, some will choose (and I use that word intentionally) to add the liability of pain, regret, and stress to each failure because that's the weight they've chosen to give to it as a default or habit.

Sometimes it appears easier and more comfortable to wallow in the failure than it is to rethink, regroup, and get immediately back in the game. So the choice becomes, am I going to hang out and stay stuck in the failure, or am I going to allocate that same pain and discomfort to get back in the game? It's a question of emotional energy appropriation. It takes the same volume of mental, emotional, and physical energy in both cases, so the question becomes, Where will I put it? In hope, or hopelessness? This is the difference between being a victor or victim when failure happens.

> In life, there is no failure, just feedback. Unless you are a cook, then you get the food back. ☺

From experience, I know it can be difficult to change the way we view failure, but not changing our view and not investing the time to bring the right context will always be more difficult, harmful, and last a great deal longer. It can be challenging to re-paradigm failures because often we try to remove something negative without having something of greater value to replace it with. So the strategy here is not that we should eliminate the negative thoughts we have about failure, but move to permanently install new thinking that embraces the value found in new frames of reference—ones that will bring an ease to failure, and knowledge that every failure held in the right light is nothing more than success in disguise.

Own a NEW position on breakdown, failures, mistakes, and missteps today.

57. Defining your own brand of business etiquette is a best practice. Stop wasting time contemplating what is right, what is wrong, and who you are.

Google "business etiquette" and you'll get about 11.2 million hits. Obviously, I'm not alone in my observations about etiquette. Breathing is the only prerequisite necessary to be aware that there is a massive decrease in common courtesies in the business world today. Lack of follow-through, calls not returned, delayed responses, inappropriate comments or behaviors, being late to meetings, and the list goes on—all of it degrading, destroying, distracting, delaying, and disrupting relationships and progress.

Business etiquette is one of those rarely talked about opportunities to quickly move into a standout brand within our companies and solidify our reputation with our peers. Little thought, however, goes into what our own style of day-to-day etiquette should look like, the impact it could make, and how it would reflect on our image, because too often we are caught up in the chaos of simply getting through the day. And yet etiquette, well executed, can reduce chaos to a pile of rubble and make the day a wonderful thing to inhabit.

> Good etiquette doesn't do average: it goes beyond average to deliver an experience that will be respected, remembered, and ultimately rewarded.

At its core, business etiquette is a designed system of behaviors and responses that will govern who you'll be in your job, which will ultimately define the brand you are. It will also clarify the way you go about doing business and drill into the specifics of how you will relate to, respect, and deal with people. Although we're held to a specific standard of performance relating to our job titles (and often defined in our job description), there is little (if any) attention and generally no training given to one of the biggest career-impacting attributes of our brand. It is generally expected that our job performance should be at par, so others will rarely notice a job done at status quo. What they will notice is the excellence we employ *beyond the basic job*. These are the things that stand out and move us to the front of the line when good things are happening.

So where to start? Every job is unique. We have to design the system that works for us: one we can live with, one we believe creates a clear window into our character, one that allows us to go beyond what is expected and make things better at work. For example, here's mine:

1. Call everyone back the same day.
2. Remember people's names and a little something about them.
3. Stay off digital devices when in social circumstances, unless I ask permission.
4. Pay vendors more than their invoice when they do an amazing job.
5. Don't just keep commitments: make ones that call me to a higher level of performance and fulfill them.
6. Listen to others with intentionality and avoid thinking of other things, losing eye contact, or being distracted.
7. If seated, stand when being introduced.
8. Appreciate others for doing a job well.
9. Begin conversations by focusing on the other and end conversations politely.

The nice part about having your own defined system is that you will no longer have to use intellectual energy contemplating whether you should say certain things or act out certain behaviors because they will be habitual, sustained by the value they create.

> You don't treat others with respect just because they deserve it; you treat others with respect because you deserve it.

So how do you tell if etiquette is working? It's simple, but it requires paying attention and being honest with yourself. Sometimes when we go the extra mile and exemplify etiquette we believe is valuable, we assume that others should respond a certain way. To measure etiquette is to simply look at what shows up in others as we bring our form of etiquette to them. If we see smiles, we're on the right track, if they share gratefulness and positive affirmation in the form of kind words or gestures or returned responses of some kind, we're doing well. If you see anything other than something positive, be cognizant that your etiquette is not faring well. And if results are less than desirable, a little inquiry will help with what's working and what's not.

Design your own system of etiquette today and give it a go.

58. It matters a great deal when we get distracted by things that don't really matter.

Several years ago during a fairly challenging economic time, I was sitting down with a CEO who was having serious business challenges. Sales were down, and her marketing plan was not functioning according to strategy. I asked her to *tell me more* and she eventually got vulnerable and shared she felt bankruptcy was looming just around the corner. Not a good place to be. Obviously, I was there to discuss sales and marketing strategy, but I wanted to get a pulse on where her commitment was to the business, as the work I do goes beyond tools and tactics into refocusing beliefs and dealing with strongholds. In light of asking strategic questions that reveal what needs to be exposed, I asked her an obscure question, "So what kinds of things are you reading these days?" She shared that she was reading a really good romance novel. Knowing we had a trusted relationship and that I could share honestly, I said, "Perhaps you might want to consider reading something on sales and marketing as it relates to the business predicament you're in. With over a hundred employees, there's nothing romantic about a bankruptcy for you or all the families under your care." For a split second, she looked like she'd been hit by a train, then she smiled and acknowledged she'd been busted (in a good way). We also discovered there were other distractions in place that were systemic and in need of being dealt with immediately.

> These days, with business as hard as it is, it is easy to medicate ourselves with distraction.

The whole idea of distractions smacks me firsthand, because as a CEO there were *many* times I would medicate myself with distraction and not focus on the hard issues because they seemed too difficult to deal with. The more I avoided what was essential, the more difficult things became, and the more lives were affected because of it. The more I escaped confronting things head-on, the worse my brand became in my agency. There were multiple prices I paid for my distractions, and yet the second (and I do mean second) I decided to start working on the critical versus veering toward the comfortable, optimism surfaced, I was driven by a new inventory of motivation, and things changed for me within a very short time. It was as immediate as a decision.

> Focused thought on a work issue will always be assaulted by distraction. The volume of focus on the matter will always be proportional to its resolution.

Every day at your work there are primary things that need to get done and there are ancillary things that could perhaps be postponed or delegated to someone. But then there are those "other" distractions like hopping online and getting our social fix, looking at cars, clothes, sports . . . *whatever*. Since I am one who is easily distracted, I wanted to learn more about this debilitating corporate disease, so I engaged in conversations with dozens of professionals by asking a simple question: What are some of the things you do or distractions you engage in that keep you from the primary work you need to be doing daily? Without going into the laundry list of work-avoidance strategies I uncovered (and there were many), I will tell you that every professional has a repertoire of distractions that keep them from achieving the things that they know they need to get done. Meanwhile, others look on and wonder, *Why am I working so hard while they drift into Distractionville?*

Strategically, there's probably 10–20 percent, perhaps even upwards of 30 percent, of extra time available in our days by eliminating any distractions that we migrate to because we need a little comfort here and there. I'm not saying to *not* have planned points of rest during the day, just telling you that the abuse of distraction demands an honest conversation with ourselves about how much time we are wasting and how much it is affecting our personal brand and success at work.

Eliminate the things that mean little and see how capacity increases a lot today.

59. What if you didn't judge people for who they currently are, but helped them in the process of who they are becoming?

Just a guess, but right now at work or in life there are certain people who rub you wrong, whom you can't stand, or whom you've got pegged in some negative light. There's a chance your judgment of them might be spot-on discernment for who they are, how they perform, and the liability they may be to you and/or the organization. Or perhaps you're off base or have a biased view founded on your previous experiences with others who seem like them.

The main issue here is not whether you're right or wrong: this is one of those cases where either way, holding someone in a negative light casts a shadow on your brand, and your voice in their life will be filtered with skepticism and guardedness if you hold a disposition of judgment over them. Your voice in their life will lose influence, and any desire to impact or move them in a positive way will be viewed as a threat or as something done out of manipulation.

There's an alternative perspective by which to view people—not necessarily in light of where they are at today, but in light of *who they are becoming* (perhaps even with your help). If we choose, we can live in such a place of self-control that rather than allowing people to irritate us and steal a percentage of our precious positive emotion, we can choose to take the opportunity to encourage them on their journey of life, help them, and better them. You could even say these people are a provision to help us to become better teachers, encouragers, and supporters of others—a very valuable asset for anyone looking to further their professional aspirations.

One thing is certain: we never quite know what people have endured in their life, why they are the way they are or do the things they do. Case in point: many years ago I was driving down the road and a guy was weaving into my lane. At the next stoplight I requested he roll down his window and told him to learn how to drive. He apologized and told me (along with a few expletives) he had just lost his wife in a car accident, and he rolled his window up. That was an important moment for me to understand that I never know the whole story of people—their past, their hurts, fears, and wounds—and it became a mission for me to help people as opposed to judging them in my ignorance and immaturity.

> Those who place judgment on other people know not who they are. Their identity is created solely by comparison to others.

I don't know about you, but if I look back at my own life, at who I was ten or twenty years ago, I'd say I'm a remarkably different person today than I was then. I can also say without question there were serious areas that needed to be worked on, and there were those in my life who stood with me holding optimism about who I would become instead of who I was at the time. In other words, they showed grace for my current condition and helped me get into better shape—not by judging me, but through working with me, teaching me, and having candid conversations without condemnation. These people hold a very special place in my heart, and there is nothing I would not do for them and no way that I would not help them. Their brand with me has equity for life, and even if they did mess up with me at some point, the value of their impact on my life would overshadow the breakdown. That's how powerful it is when people stand for growth in our life instead of silently condemning us.

Every day, be patient and support people in who they are becoming; they may do the same with you.

60. Asking better questions is the answer to having better conversations.

Ask any human if they'd like to be 10–50 percent smarter at work tomorrow without any cost, with very little effort, and with guaranteed fun—you'd have people lining up around the planet. And if you asked anyone if they'd like to increase the effectiveness of what they say while reducing the quantity of inaccurate, uninspiring, unproductive, and (let's be bold here) idiotic things they say, the line would be just as long. *I'd be in it.* This reality is possible, but it requires becoming proficient in asking great questions, aka *strategic inquiry.* It's a learned skill, and becoming equipped with an arsenal of great questions and a predisposition of curiosity is the quickest path to business and social intelligence I've ever seen.

The challenge in conversations is that we can become so self-focused thinking about what great thing we're going to say or do next that we miss the critical subtleties of the conversation. The result? We end in a one-way broadcast. Yet the real value of our contribution is found in staying in tune with the conversation and leveraging the use of relevant questions so we can operate from a place of *wisdom* instead of gambling with our rhetoric.

I'm somewhat of an expert on this issue. For a good part of my life and career I was more concerned about what I was going to say than what I might have learned by asking great questions. I didn't know the full extent of the malady until I discovered the relational equity and productivity that was found in clearing my mind to listen, clarify, and ask great questions instead of being captive to an odd pressure to say something smart while being labeled as uninterested, uncaring, and uncool. There is a peace found in the conversation that relaxes the mind when we are using inquiry to its full potential.

> The more relevant questions we ask, the smarter we become. It's really that simple.

The fact is, conversations will always be awkward if we are busy thinking about what we're going to say. When we're thinking about our next comment, we often disembark from the exchange, missing key details that would give us the right ammunition to fire the perfect bullet of guidance, feedback, and value. Instead we tend to shotgun out pressured comments that spray on everybody, and if lucky, hit part of the target. Most often, the comments generally fall on deaf ears or polarize the room without the results we're looking for. Either way, conversational momentum slows or stops with these kinds of comments, and the only things we receive back are silence and blank stares. The outcome ultimately can harm our brand.

If we invested in the habit of curiosity versus the habit of self-focus, our communication, contributions, and personal brand would improve socially and professionally—*instantly*. There would be more natural, less-forced communications that would create a conversational ease with more value inquiring in rather than stressing out. But there is an art to being curious just like there is an art to making statements; both require focused listening and a commitment to serve rather than impress. As a side note, there is such a thing as a stupid question, and it generally shows up when someone is not listening very well and instead is asking a question regarding something they should have already been in tune with if they hadn't checked out.

> The creativity of your questions will drive the trajectory of your conversations.

Just like we build a library of great books to be more attuned to life and success, we can build a library of great questions. For example, when I meet with a client who desires to build a great brand, I have a preset list of questions that are process driven to give me all the feedback I need to be valuable to the client with the least chance of missing the mark. And generally before the meeting I will scrub and adjust the list: every client is different, so I will generally add several customized questions. If I'm only naming a company, I have a list for that as well. Lots of lists because I need lots of information. For the most part, the greater the inquiry, the more confident the client will be that I am in touch with their needs, the market, and how best to achieve success. Even when I meet with someone over lunch to get feedback on something I need help with, I generally do the same thing: create a list of questions that focus the conversation to get the best results. Plus, it honors the person who is taking the time to help.

> Our value is more often known by the questions we ask than the statements that we make.

Become good enough at asking questions and you'll always have some at the ready. They're the ones you know drive greater clarity, opportunity, and enjoyment into conversations. One such question I use when working with individuals when we've discovered a breakdown in behavior of some sort is, "Where else does this behavior show up in your life?" Sometimes they'll reveal so many areas where the behavior causes havoc that I don't have to say a word to improve their situation. The question became the answer. The bottom line is that life, business, and relationships will be proportionally better contingent on the number of great questions we have in our inventory. As a friend of mine once said, "Never underestimate the gift of a great question."

Ask better questions to have a better life today.

61. Being "different" used to be the big thing. Different can still be good but relevant is far better.

Regarding products, services, or even people, there was a time when being different had great value. Something or someone new came along, and we all took notice and thought there must be something valuable here because it was *different*. Intrigue alone was enough to create interest, convincing us this was something we should have even though we knew little about the elixir that cured all illness, the app that fixed everything, the fitness machine that gave us six-pack abs, or the president that promised change.

Today "different" is all around us. Different is becoming more homogenized every day as we live in a "world of different." Media channels have made us so keenly aware that different exists that, in some ways, being different is being categorized as normal. So why do we strive to be different?

There are many drivers of wanting to be unique. The desire to be noticed. The fear of blending in or being the same. It may be an "anti" position in defiance of a multitude of things. Could just be that we don't like what we see in certain others: "I don't want to be like Mom, Dad, my co-workers, my brother, my sister, my boss," or whoever. Candidly, the motive of wanting to be different can be a self-centered stance that causes such alienation from others that it's worth looking at the actual value of what various forms of different get you. There's a relatable difference that wears in over time and has some merit, and then there's a completely unrelatable, unconnectable difference that wears out before it even gets started.

> Differentiation is not valued for how much it
> deviates, but how much it captivates.

The more relatable, success-focused approaches to different—such as standing out from the norm, being the best in your category, and doing something like no one else—are better than the alternatives. But regardless of where the motivation comes from, different will always be risky, and it's wise to assess the potential payoff versus the potential put-off of being different if you decide to go down that road. Case in point: one of my clients in the technology business built a software platform and was convinced that the main features of their new program would be successful because nobody else on the market had them. We built the brand and all the messaging and campaigns around these differentiated features, launched the product, and what did we hear back? Nothing but crickets. The phone didn't ring, the sales team was frustrated, and although the campaign shared the message succinctly, their difference lacked one key ingredient—*relevance*. Although the features were of some value, it became obvious that our client's idea of "valuable" was different from what the market wanted. But since we were hired well after the product was developed, we didn't have the opportunity to recommend the client conduct product research to find out if different was going to be compatible with the demands of the market and make sense . . . as well as sales.

> Today, relevant is the new different.

Although software is a product example, our own brand demands the same consideration. Is our focus on being rarified or different based in relevancy to bring specific value to specific situations, or is it driven by an ulterior motive? In other words, will our desire to be different be more fad-like, passing with little attention to it and lacking in sustained benefit for those who experience it? Or will we replace the mindset of standing *out* from the crowd and being noticed, with standing *for* the crowd and being respected? Relevant is the new different, and it's wise to do a check-in every now and then as to our relevance at home, work, or wherever we are on a regular basis. Of course, if relevance requires being different, then be different—in *that light*. But never sacrifice relevance for difference, otherwise you'll find yourself in need of something . . . well, *different*.

Discover what your relevance is and make that your mark today.

62. Social media done well means business.

In an earlier point I briefly covered some danger points of social media as it relates to our online brand. On the philosophical side, I want to share some of the things I've learned that will help your brand become and stay relevant if you chose to get social for work purposes. It's entirely different from being social for social purposes and provides opportunities that go beyond the cat video or picture of a birthday cake.

There are dozens of social business channels to consider engaging with. Obviously you're not going to have time to engage with a dozen social channels, so researching and choosing the top one or two you have time for and purposing to establish and maintain a presence on those will be key to getting a return on your investment that you can measure over time. To select the audience you'd like to communicate with, just imagine if you could have a roomful of people to present to for the purposes of furthering your career: Who would be in the room? Once you've identified those people, find out where they congregate and communicate. That's your channel, and if your audience adjusts over time, change channels to adapt. Once you find the right group(s), nose around a bit and check the basic communication protocol, content, and style so you can hit the ground relating instead of agitating.

> Social media channels for business have little grace and an extraordinary memory. Write well or be written off.

Social media *is* one place where first impressions make a huge difference, so I'd suggest developing a simple one-page plan for yourself on how you'll approach the audience, what you're going to communicate over the course of a calendar year, and the brand you'll want to create with those there. It's important to be focused. Typically, a generalist who bounces from subject to subject will be less likely to be noticed than someone who is known for something specific and compelling. Also, stay on point with your communication so the channel can connect and relate to what you write. Business-related social channels are not places to sound off on personal views, nor to take unnecessary risks to stand out. They are places where you deliver clear "within the guidelines" value with every post consistent with the theme or focus. As for *quality* versus *quantity* of content, it's a no-brainer. A truckload of mediocre isn't nearly as powerful as small special deliveries of compelling content—meaning never post something on a social channel that is not your best work. It's the kiss of death to your brand to post average content, and a couple times doing so will have people scrolling by and saying goodbye . . . in some cases, permanently.

It's no secret that engaging in comments and conversations online can be dangerous, as the online world is devoid of audible tone, facial indicators, and rapid responses for recovery, if needed. It's also subject to diverse interpretation, and often words given little thought and delivered at the speed of response can do serious damage to your reputation in the channel. Think through what you write in conversations, reread them, and place yourself on the other side of them. It's often in the revisits that you'll see potential conflicts that can be smoothed over while still getting your message across. It's not always what you say in social media that hurts you, but how you say it.

> Social media is in its infancy. Those who learn it and learn it well will dominate with the least-costly, highest-impact marketing medium ever available to the general public.

Make sure that you are statistically and factually correct in all that you write. It helps to reference any callouts that are fact based as it adds to the credibility of your brand and keeps you from negative comments and potentially being asked to leave the group. If you post something you've heard or read, you can research it online; if you can't find it, just note it was something that you came across. Quick disclaimers such as "Something I heard at a workshop" or "This is just my opinion, not fact" to cover any point made are appreciated. This way you're covered to a degree.

Every day, more social media channels are opening up; although social media is relatively new compared to traditional mediums, it's wise to become proficient with it, just like it's wise to become a good swimmer if you're going to take up sailing. Having spent tens of millions of dollars of client money to build both personal and business brands, I can say without question that this medium will be the most efficient method of communication in the future to improve our brand and impact our business, if done well.

Identify the social channels that make sense for you and start thinking of ways to communicate via those channels to improve the lives of others today.

63. Brilliant actors rehearse for a play. Brilliant business people rehearse for their day.

I'm astonished at the repetitiveness I can live in daily. Especially in the morning. The alarm clock rings and I cut through my routine like a chainsaw through a pencil. Before I know it I'm sitting down at my computer getting hit with who knows what and no idea of what's around the corner. I've given zero thought to who I'm going to be today or how I'm going to act, and I've given little thought to what and who is in the day. I've invested little in the way of preparing my heart and mind for the people I will see, conversations I will have, problems I might encounter, and more. It's like I drop myself straight into the middle of a war zone unprepared for the day. These are the days when everything I do catches me by surprise, and I find myself fearing and struggling my way through the day I created by my choices. The next day comes, the alarm clock rings, and I do it all over again.

This was a snapshot of me before I met a guy named Derek . . .

> If you think upon a good thought long enough
> it will end up a good thing. Just a good thought
> I had . . . soon to be a good thing.

Many years ago I sat down for breakfast with Derek, a mentor to CEOs. I had no idea what that meant or what to expect. Honestly, I wasn't expecting much, which reveals my level of skepticism or arrogance at the time. After a few interesting questions, he asked me to share about a typical day. I basically described the first paragraph of this chapter you just read. Then he said, "Tell me about today." He caught me off guard. My words were as fragmented as a politician with a broken teleprompter. Next, he pointed out two things that changed my life radically. First, he said, you don't attack your day with a clear vision; you stumble into it and end up a pinball. I just about fell out of the booth laughing. He'd nailed me right between the eyes. Most days by about 10:00 I was bouncing all over the place with no clear direction, again pushing my way through the day contending with most things as a surprise rather than a well-planned or thought-out event. The second thing he shared was so powerful it had me paralyzed in the booth almost crying. He said—and I'll never forget it—"The people around you don't get to experience the full gift that you are every day because you don't care enough about them to prepare for the day. They experience a half-present, scattered, dealing-on-the-fly guy who doesn't have the inclination or capacity to add value to others . . . others, by the way, who in some way are a means to your end and not the other way around." By this time he had my attention (by the throat) and it was one of the more valuable learning lessons of my life.

> A few seconds of semi-focused thought on a topic is generally useless. Real revelation comes from two or three minutes of highly focused, uninterrupted contemplation.

The takeaway from that day was profound, yet simple. Basically, I would sit down with my schedule and spend 10–15 minutes going through the day to get clear about my emotional disposition for the day and for meetings I had with certain people. I began to role-play some of the conversations in my mind that I knew would be more difficult or important. I considered what my presence would be with others, the attitude I would bring into the day, how I would listen, and how I would engage with others. I envisioned the day from start to finish, including my time at home. The potential in this process makes it among the most valuable disciplines we can practice.

There's something special about going to work knowing that you've already invested focused thought into what you will be exposed to when you get there. It creates a confidence that improves every aspect of the workday and will give you an edge to perform your job at a higher level while bringing relationships to new places. Although this process remains one of my best life practices, I have to confess I don't do it every day, just days that I want to be more confident, competent, and effective. It's a practice I categorize as one of those immediately accessible, real-life, real-time advantages.

Take a bit of time to think through the entirety of your workday today and who you will be in it.

64. If you want to quickly improve the response to your brand at work, respond to others more quickly.

One of the most commonly overlooked brand attributes required to keep pace with the frenetic reality of business today is not just follow-through when responding, but the *speed of response*. Just about every day those we work with dispense verbal or written commitments such as, "I'll get back to you"; "I'll call you back ASAP"; "You'll have it Tuesday, I promise"; "I'll let you know"; and so on. Well, there are some people we trust to respond within reason and others where it feels like a trip to Vegas, a call to a bookie, and placing odds on the time they'll take to get back—if they get back at all. These are the kind of people who can benefit a team by leaving it, and soon they will. It's sad but true. If you think about the last several customer service experiences that you had with providers, then you've probably experienced a level of responsiveness that is approaching ridiculous in terms of quality, which means the bar is pretty low and the opportunity to stand out is apparent. And it just so happens that of all the ways you improve your brand at work, quick responsiveness is at the top of the pile.

> When it comes to your responsiveness as a team player, are your response times more of a nervous question mark or an inspiring exclamation point?

In some ways, a book like this can be overwhelming when you think about how many things it calls you to do to be a great brand.

175

It only seems that way because if you add up the to-do list elements of this book it's a few hundred potential brand-value points. But the to-dos, like responding quickly, are again driven from a simple way of being. Having just a few character traits on more of a "to-be" list will drive an infinite number of to-dos on your to-do list without you having to think about it, plan for it, or work toward it.

One of those ways of being, as I've mentioned before, is the attribute of genuinely valuing people: considering the totality of their lives as meaningful to you, understanding that behind what you see at work is a life full of roles, responsibilities, and challenges—*just like you have.* The more you get in touch with this, the more you'll be inclined to respond quickly and thoroughly to those you work with. You'll end up respecting others in ways that will fast-track relationships to a whole new level of trust and reward. I'm not sure if you've ever read the Bible, but there is incredible brilliance in that book; one concept it teaches is that there's tangible value and progress in counting others as more important than ourselves.

To really appreciate the value of responsiveness, you have to think of how it feels when people react quickly to your request, handle your problem, or fill an unmet need. It's pretty astonishing, because we don't really expect it. We've grown to tolerate that it's the norm for people to get back to us when they're good and ready, and that "far beyond our control" feeling that accompanies the norm is way too common and frankly unnecessary. By simply refusing to accept vague commitments that are absent of timeline and detail, you'll be able to ensure a greater percentage of response. Even better, create a habit of keeping others accountable, and they will know it's just not worth it to miss a deadline with you. For example, if someone says they'll get back to you ASAP or tomorrow, simply ask what ASAP means, what specific time tomorrow, or request a "no later than" time frame so there's some specificity in play. This way your workflow isn't stifled nor are your commitments—and your brand won't be left in the hands of a blurred promise.

Give those around you the gift of a specific, rapid response, and request the same from others today.

65. Every day we talk to ourselves a thousand times more than we talk to others. Are those internal conversations adding to our success at work, slowing it down, or stopping it?

A mind has habits, and our minds left to think negatively *will not mind if you don't mind over your mind*. Like software, that little voice inside our head (LVIH) is command central on our mood, attitude, and behaviors. It is highly programmable, but it helps to understand the mechanics of the mind so we can take ownership and control of our mind instead of allowing our mind to always control us.

Most people don't realize it, but *that* voice—the one that is consistently assessing, evaluating, questioning, and judging—actually has physiological and chemical mechanisms that activate while we think, which makes the voice more impactful than we give it credit. In fact, what we think in our minds can actually record itself in our brains as if the event actually happened and bring with it the repercussions that we would normally experience if that event had *actually* occurred. This is the power of our mind, a mind we choose to be in control of, *or not*.

> A mindset of limitations is not filled with brain cells, but prison cells.

Some call the LVIH the *inner voice*; others call it the *subconscious* or *conscious mind*; and others label it our *conscience*—while others call it a *pain in the* . . . For the sake of simplicity, let's just say if we think things in our conscious mind (or basic daily thought) repetitively enough, those thoughts end up etched at some level into our subconscious mind. Metaphorically, the things we think in our conscious thought are clay to work with, and if we think those same thoughts repeatedly, they end up as *cement*. For the sake of reality, I'd like to remove the word "little" from the LVIH acronym, because "little" is a gross understatement. People label it as "little" due to its quiet, subtle, clandestine way of navigating our attitudes, emotions, and life. A better term—one that would get us comfortable with the magnitude of what we are dealing with—is the Voice That Drives Everything. Maintaining this perspective will have us thinking thoughts with the intentionality necessary to start reinventing our thought life. It's a process that will move the patterns of our mind to resemble pinstripes moving congruently in a clear direction in contrast to plaid, chaotically scrambling everywhere. Plaid thinking or pinstripe thinking. It's a matter of which direction you'd like to head with the Voice in Your Head (VIH).

The starting point for gaining control over our thoughts is to separate the brain from the mind. The brain is basically the physical mass through which we think. It's the hard drive, meaning without programming it is useless and will do nothing. The software is our mind, and we are the programmer who has complete control as to what we allow or install on the hard drive and how we deal with it once it's programmed there. As the programmer, we can be casual about thought, even catatonic, or we can be focused and calculated, bringing much-needed governance and much-wanted mastery over the one thing that rules over everything.

> That which you give your mind to will
> consume you—good or bad!

During our workday we may have thoughts like, "I'm not good enough for that"; "it's not going to turn out well"; "the project is going to fail"; "we're not going to win the deal"; "I'm not going to get the promotion"; "it's probably not my time"; and countless more. The strange thing is that in some cases these are not even fully formed thoughts but more like halfway between a feeling and a thought, fragmented and incomplete. The reason they don't need to manifest into a fully formed thought to do damage is that the buildup of bad thinking creates a feeling or tone that begins to solidify into our thoughts, personality, and actions. This is the cement I was talking about earlier. When enough negative feelings and thoughts go astray for a while, hopelessness, depression, and anxiety can set in like concrete. Which takes us back to the clay stage—the time when thoughts are best dealt with.

As it relates to a negative thought life, the Bible addresses the importance of taking every thought that doesn't serve you *captive*. The word *captive* means keeping your enemy at the point of stillness using the tip of a spear at the jugular vein. That's the intensity it demands, as the enemy is a negative thought that can take you out with a quiet violence that would rival anything physical. As strange as this sounds, visualize putting a gate on your mind, a gate that keeps negative thoughts from getting in. You now have a gate. You are the designated gatekeeper. You control what goes in and out, and you've been given every tool needed to do this job at a high level of proficiency with absolute consistency if you so choose. As thoughts approach the gate, take note that your thought isn't your identity, just something formed from experiences, upbringing, beliefs, etc. This allows you to release the contained thought as merely a "thing" and not something macro, as if the thought is *who you are*. If thoughts make it through the gate (and they will), it is designed to keep the thought contained inside until you can repurpose it into something that works. Never be without a gate, a fence, a wall, or whatever metaphor works for you to keep crap-like thinking out of your game. The barrier is designed to protect you from thoughts running wild and removing the shine from your brand.

Take a few negative thoughts captive and replace them with new thinking that strengthens you today.

66. Success is a rhythm. Scheduled meetings that fail to happen for no good reason kill that rhythm.

Ever show up at a restaurant or coffeehouse meeting only to wait some arbitrary amount of time before you call the missing party to discover they forgot, didn't have it on their schedule, or thought it was next week? It happens all the time. I see people waiting around, staring at their watches, looking at everyone who comes through the door, checking their phones, going outside to make a call, coming back in to give it one last try, looking at the door again, and then with one last glance at their watch, getting up and walking out. *No show, rhythm stopped!*

> It reflects well on our brand when we confirm things. It gives others a sense of confidence that we care.

Many busy professionals have no less than six to ten meetings a week. That's 300 to 500 meetings per year. Whether internal or external, there's meeting preparation, an emotional investment, and irretrievable time associated with every meeting, pre-, mid-, and post-meeting. Of course meetings get missed. I know from experience. It happened to me no less than several hundred times in my career until I took note of a valuable personal statistic: nearly every meeting I confirmed in advance actually happened. I discovered that a two-step process works best:

1. The day before the meeting, I text around 10:30 AM confirming time, place, and parameters of meeting.
2. Next day, first thing, I send a quick text and sometimes an email saying something like, "Looking forward to seeing you today at [this place], at [this time]."

Even though today's technology helps minimize scheduling hiccups, confirming meetings is a great best practice you'll benefit from, and one others will appreciate. I'm amazed at how many meeting confirmations yield the comment, "Dean, I'm glad you confirmed, I totally forgot." So it's either 30–60 seconds to confirm and have it happen, and keep the rhythm, or risk not confirming and potentially lose valuable work time, miss the meeting, have to re-prepare, and reset the meeting.

Confirm the meetings you have every time, as time is the currency of business.

67. Mistakes should fuel us forward, not fail us backward.

We will make mistakes in our careers: some small, some large, some embarrassing, some of which will have notable impact on others. There are mistakes that will blindside us, while others we had a feeling might be coming due to decisions we made. But knowing that the most successful people on the planet have made more mistakes than the rest by a long shot, we should frame mistakes to fuel us forward, not fail us backward. Mistakes can be painful. I know from experience, I've made many. They can throw us into self-judgment, fear, uncertainty about our future, and worst of all, into mental inventions of what others might be thinking and thoughts that keep us up at night.

> Knowledge isn't power until it becomes action. When it becomes action, it often creates mistakes; when it creates mistakes, it becomes wisdom; when it becomes wisdom . . . then knowledge creates power.

There are two different types of mistakes. There are *careless mistakes*, often characterized by simply not caring enough to maintain a cautious disposition (hence the wording, "care less"). These kinds of mistakes are tolerated once or twice and *do not* reflect well on our brand, as the mistake itself is far less of an issue than the lack of care. When people see that the care component is missing, you'll be branded as a liability waiting to happen, and no one needs people around like that to add to their stress level or have a negative effect on *their* brand.

Then there are *pioneering mistakes*: mistakes made while exploring new possibilities, taking risks to have something great happen, or taking a chance and doing something no one else has attempted in order to better the business in some way. As a CEO, I have never been upset with someone in my company trying something risky if it will better the company. Instead, I honor the person for trying, show appreciation, then do some discovery and give counsel for better results in the future. If a person "Lone Rangers" it, I'll generally tell them that it's good to let others know what you're up to in advance of the move and get feedback for blind spots as well as how you can better the idea while mitigating the risk. But this is something you want to do prior to execution, and you'll need to check results along the way. Then, if you're called to account for weaker results than expected, you'll have covered the bases of collaboration and measurement, which reflects well on you.

> If you have the courage to admit when you're
> wrong, you'll be right 100 percent of the time.

Mistakes do not need to be painful if we accept the fact that they are a necessary, ongoing part of success. We can hold them with the weight of a feather instead of a sledgehammer, knowing that everyone who has ever achieved anything of substance sees mistakes as motivation, not devastation, and simply part of the process. Mistakes as a tool are a key asset to our learning that will accelerate our acumen in business more than any other method. Nothing comes close.

The core principle behind your brand staying intact when you make a mistake is to own up to it *instantly* and *confidently*. Don't try to manipulate the conversation or skirt the issue. Give those on the other end of your breakdown the courtesy of sharing the truth about what happened and why. And, of course, never place blame on anyone who isn't in the room with you, as that doesn't reflect well on taking ownership of the mistake and will be viewed as gossip. Lastly, when any mistake discussion is coming to a close, genuinely (and I mean sincerely) ask those involved for forgiveness for what you caused, and let them know it will not happen again. Then watch the stress dissipate before your eyes.

See your mistakes as progress and opportunity, not regress and liability, today.

68. You are uniquely brilliant, with an incredible ability to impact others' lives with the gift that you are, in all areas of life.

If you think about what makes something successful, it's the collective mindshare of every person involved: their talents, gifting, and spin on things. No workplace or venture is successful without a mix of people, and the mix is diverse. On one hand you have innovator types, prolific in what they create, who anguish at the mere sight of a spreadsheet (that's me). Then you have those who can look at a wall full of numbers and save the company from disaster, but can't draw a stick man or write a solid sentence to save their lives. In addition, there are people who can work hand-in-hand with Type-A control freaks but don't work well with analytical people, and others who can work well with people who have learning disabilities where others would lose patience in forty-five seconds. We are all equally different, but brilliant in our own specific way, *all with something to offer—inside the workplace and out.*

I've had the benefit of being with many who use their unique gifts and abilities to serve people in need outside the workplace. They don't charge for it; they simply see they can offer value to others based on what they've learned thus far in their lives and careers. The truth is, there are always others who will benefit from more knowledge and guidance, especially from those with experience rather than book knowledge. There is something very special about these givers because their life has added balance, refinement, and purpose built in that *all of them* have claimed are the more rewarding parts of their life. Although this activity takes only about 3–5 percent of their time, they say giving casts a bright light on their life that they would never be without.

This idea goes back to that personal mission statement that I shared earlier. Mine, as you may remember, is "to be a graceful interruption to things that don't work in people's lives, both personally and professionally." So as a closet counselor, businessman, and branding guy, I've found groups and other channels with whom I share my set of abilities. I also put the word out to parents of 18- to 30-year-olds that I really enjoy coaching as it relates to career, and I have regular calls from people who've heard about my work. I've done it so consistently over the years that I no longer have to mention it. It comes at just the right time and in just the right amount so it works within my schedule and I don't get burned out.

> We are born into a body only to someday leave it—
> keeping nothing we attain in this life except for what we
> give. Therefore giving now is the gift we can all share.

There's a great book out called *Half Time* by Bob Buford. The premise of the book is that when we reach some level of achievement in our careers, it's time to move from that achievement to significance (e.g., the things we're talking about here, deeper and more meaningful things). But without significance integrated into our life, success is impossible, and therefore the *Half Time* reality, although valuable, is an unfortunate default for those who want to have true success from the beginning of their careers. I believe our gifts and abilities should be integrated into our life application early in our careers as opposed to "sometime down the road." That way when we're at the halftime of our life, we can accelerate our impact with more time, resources, and historical precedence than we would have if we'd started that journey from scratch at halftime.

Many people I talk to will tell me they don't know where to start giving. I respond with, "Of course you do, but you've just never given it a concentrated dose of thought or the research needed to see what's available and what's possible." The clubs, associations, groups, people types, hospitals, charities, and needs in this world are endless. A little soul-searching may help you find that perfect fit to use your gifts and abilities for good. It's crazy but true that people offered the opportunity to give of themselves have been brought out of things like loneliness, depression, and anxiety. Some have even stopped criminal behavior when given the opportunity to (believe it or not) care for an animal. The same holds true with an opportunity to help people of all kinds. Although we are giving of ourselves, our time, and our abilities, often *we* are the ones who get the most from the involvement. It's fun to give, and it's even more enjoyable when you have a consistent place to do it. It's a break from our busy lives that somehow gives us more fuel to *contend* with our busy lives and adds incomparable value to living.

Give some thought to how you can give the brand of brilliance that you are to others today.

69. When you enter a room, your appearance speaks long before you do.

A big part of our brand presence shows up in what we wear. Unfortunately, most people visit a clothing store, choose not to ask for help, and pick outfits that may feel like they fit well but would actually look better back on the rack from which they came. It's like spinning the roulette wheel and hoping for a good outcome. This type of gambling approach creates more losing scenarios than winners. But with online fashion sites, articles, and pictures that fit and/or complement every body type, demographic, skin tone, and hair color, there's no excuse for not having a wardrobe that says, *I thought this through*.

> Clothes are what we buy, but style is what
> we create with what we buy.

I always thought an important asset was to look professional and to make an impression. So as a young executive I bartered a trade deal with a clothier and ended up with a custom wardrobe. My guy made suggestions for fabrics and styles that were more suited toward his vision than mine, but he told me to trust him. Long story short, I ended up with a closetful of clothes I felt awkward wearing. They were creative and well put together, but I felt inauthentic in them and eventually gave them away to charity. I did this again many years later with Rod Alan, a custom clothier, and we collectively looked at the total picture and crafted a wardrobe that I would wear consistently when business scenarios called for it.

> Well-coordinated clothing is not just about how you look in your clothes, but the confidence you feel while wearing the clothes you're in.

The good news is, we all have eyes and imagination. We envision things we think we'd look good in but seldom do the research to confirm what colors, styles, and fabrics would work well for our brand. We all have access to great clothes at reasonable prices that can look and feel like a million bucks if chosen well. There are only a few steps to get this right. Get online, research, print pictures (if necessary), go to stores, and get some help finding what you're looking for. If you have a friend who can help or you can find a store clerk with design sense, a little help goes a long way.

Consider how what you wear can take your brand to a new level today.

70. Avoid buzzwords, catchphrases, and lines that are overly used. They make you appear canned like sardines–smelling of something fishy and looking not so lively.

How we communicate is everything. Words are the language of progress; a little forethought before speaking is a great way to protect and strengthen our brand. We've touched on this, but improving how we communicate (even if just a fractional percentage each day) can make a remarkable difference.

Buzzwords and catchphrases are things people say to appear they are current and "with it." They are also a means to contribute words without actually delivering any real value to the conversation. They resonate like nails on a chalkboard and sound something like this: "At the end of the day, guys, we need to integrate more synergy and have a more dynamic approach that will scale, because if we don't do a deep dive and think outside the box and bring a value-add, then we'll have to circle back and bring more forward thinking to the table. That being said . . ." Today, with content overabundance, buzzwords and catchphrases are so pervasive that when we hear them, they actually become a source of distraction and we disconnect from what is actually being said. Not a good thing if we want to be heard.

> Our intelligence is not measured in the brilliance of what we say, but in the simplicity of how well it's said.

Having interviewed hundreds of people, I've come across several that were completely reliant on buzzwords and catchphrases, as if they were going to impress me with the current vernacular of the day. The sad part is, I always had to break past the veneer of these plastic conversations to get to know the person, and in some cases I wasn't able to get through. I shook their hands and said goodbye, while inside thinking, *It was nice NOT getting to know you.* Very unfortunate. Conversely, the ones who resonated best were the ones who spoke plainly and rather than trying to impress me with their communication skills, simply gave a clear answer to what was being asked. There wasn't a buzzword or catchphrase to be found. That was impressive and a complete breath of fresh air.

What works today is to communicate simply—and at risk of being politically incorrect—to speak plain English. The emphasis here is on *plain* and not on *English*. Could be Spanish, French, or Farsi, for all I care. Buzzwords and catchphrases come in all languages and will always be appreciated when *absent* from conversations. Even the use of profanity is a momentary lapse of creativity in language. It shows up because we don't have a more intelligent and compelling way to communicate what it is that we want to say with such emphasis. As a result, we default to throwing out an expletive to make a point that could be made without profanity.

Stock lines (phrases and jokes that we use over and over again because back in the day they got a good laugh, made an impression, or moved the needle) are another bit of communication that comes across as either flaccid or expected. The problem is that without switching them up, they make us appear to be robotic and canned like those sardines I mentioned in the headline.

I was once in a transaction to sell a company, and the mergers-and-acquisitions specialist used words that kept everybody on point. They sounded fresh, relevant, and smart. After one of these meetings, I inquired about these words. The specialist shared that language is so important in meetings where emotions are heightened that every couple of months he connects with new words so he can keep it fresh and yet still get his points across. I found this practice to be brilliant and a great example of originating content that inspires confidence and clarity where buzzwords would bring confusion. The key here is to ignore "trendy" and communicate from the real you so you can *refine* the real you.

Take your brand to a new place of relatability by speaking at new levels of simplicity and clarity today.

71. Don't forget to stretch.

If you've ever decided to take your fitness to a new level using a coach, it would be rare if they omitted the idea of stretching in their process with you. Coaches tell us to stretch because without it, the chance of injury that would set us back or preclude us from future activity would be near certain. I know from experience: I was at the chiropractor this morning due to an injury caused from *not stretching*. The doctor told me that stretching is imperative and actually strengthens the other forms of exercise I do while muscle development and recovery are optimized. Of course as I was leaving, he said, "Don't forget to stretch." He knew that stretching would take me to a new level of capacity, and without it, I'd be back to see him in a month or two. (It's a good thing he cares more about his patient than he does about his wallet.) By the way, this was not the type of stretching I wanted to convey on this point, but thought I'd leave it in, as "flexibility strength" is the most usable form of physical strength there is. It helps us to relax and is overlooked frequently, but is very important. Just a reminder.

Let's address the stretch we do to take ourselves to new levels of accomplishment. Conceptually, it is analogous to a runner running a mile a day for a week, a mile and a half per day the following week, and two miles a day the next week, and so on. Soon they're running five miles a day five days a week, and thirteen miles on one day with a one-day rest. Before you know it, they're running half marathons, then a full marathon, competing in local races, winning . . . stretching to new levels, then trying out for the Olympic trials, and then winning a medal for distance running. This is one of many true stories that started with a commitment and a series of *stretches* but grew from a few small steps to an Olympic medal.

> Stretching ourselves to new levels will never take
> life out of us. It will, however, put it back.

So what does *stretch* mean? A speaker I once heard shared the Greek definition of the word *stretched*, derived from the word *Teneo*, which means something is stretched to the widest possible point. *Teneo* also means blessed, suggesting a gift that is bestowed upon us. It implies that when we stretch ourselves in the things we do at work and in life and we risk going for something great, there is blessing so profound in the stretch that any focus on the ramifications of failure doesn't make much sense. In fact, they become laughable in comparison to the blessing found in upping our game to improve our circumstances. It implies the bigger the risk, the greater the blessing. Common sense confirms this is true, and even if we fail, the character elevation and confidence installation should make continual risk part of our brand. Obviously we're talking about intelligent, well-thought-out risk, not flippant risk taken without consideration of counting the costs.

> If you're careful enough in life, nothing
> good or bad will ever happen to you.

You don't have to go too far to think of what a stretch might be in your career. It could be calling on that big account, having that difficult meeting with your co-worker, introducing the raise conversation with your boss, or increasing productivity by 10 percent within three months. The list is endless. Although we can understand the clear rationale behind stretch in athletics, it doesn't always show up at work, which is why a large percentage of the workforce feels like they're stuck and would bail from their current position if they could. The truth is, they can—but most are not in the habit of taking risks. Workdays devoid of risk and/or stretch will always end up in a positional atrophy and drape the color of beige over what could be a vibrant and colorful brand and life.

If you took an hour or two and outlined some risks you believe would better your position at work or improve your brand, you'd probably come up with about five to ten stretches. Put a few into action. Succeed or fail, you will see change in yourself that you can't get from reading a book, taking a pill, or going through therapy. It's that "once something is stretched, it never returns to its original form" principle, if we choose to make risk a habit.

 Gain some momentum by stretching yourself to a new level today.

72. Taking one day out of 365 to substantially improve the other 364 can make for a brilliant year.

Someone once told me I probably spend more time planning my vacations than I do planning my life. I said, "Yeah, but I have really enjoyable vacations." He was right. I didn't give much thought to my life and what I wanted to happen in it, and although I joked about it, I knew I was missing something and didn't know what. Most of the time I would just think on the fly and plan sporadically, sure that would do the trick. The truth is, by the end of the year I had no idea what it was that I planned and whether I accomplished it or not. My plan-on-the-fly thinking didn't "fly" at all—it crash-landed with consistency year after year. In retrospect, the most I ever spent planning was about fifteen minutes noodling on a particular issue with no real thinking of what I wanted to have happen, just abstract ideas and concepts without anything concrete. That changed when someone shared the concept of a planning day and gave me a simple form to fill out that paved the way to consider multiple areas of my life that hadn't been given much attention.

Work planning days are pretty amazing, and the reason is simple. Because we are taking ample time to plan and we bring intentionality to the exercise, it provides a way for us to uncover and clarify the things that we wouldn't really think about while being caught up in the chaos of just doing life. It gives our minds time to blow the dust off the old, often-ignored areas and reveals new possibilities, people, and initiatives. The time also allows our minds to reach a new level of focus to see things with greater distinctness, perspective, and hope. The openness of having a relaxed day to do this work as an opportunity to dream, contemplate, and play a bit is a stark contrast to the "cram the plan into a two-hour period because I need to get to the next thing" idea. The condensed effort will be a more mechanical, academic exercise with little emotion or spirit driven into it. The full day will provide the liberty and space to explore and drive important specificity into the who, what, why, how, and where of the plan so it becomes less obscure and more doable.

> If you want to have a brilliant year, plan to take a day so you can plan a brilliant year.

Everyone will have their own spin on what a day like this might look like. But for reference, here are a few things I integrated into mine. First, I reworked my personal mission statement and the core values I would use to achieve the things I set forth. Once the character traits were set, I broke up the rest of the categories—such as things I wanted to get done the first ninety days of the year, and so on. I had lists of habits I wanted to break and what I would replace them with. I added social goals, extended- and immediate-family goals, and some things I wanted to achieve personally that included hobbies and spiritual goals. With my businesses, I broke goals into key areas and listed the top 5 priorities for the year, numbers I wanted to achieve, people I wanted to connect with, and a miscellaneous section I could dump random thoughts into.

> Building on your career today using last year's thinking is like using an old climbing rope to climb a new mountain. Don't fall for it.

Stay connected to the plan. We all have calendars on our devices, so consider scheduling half days once a quarter; if that's too much, an hour or so to review every month could be calendared out at the beginning of the year so you can inspect progress, make adjustments, and celebrate successes. Add to that a quick weekly checkpoint of what is working and not, and you'll improve the percentages of success notably. *One day to change 364.* The math seems to add up to a sensible strategy that will bring certain measurability to what you say is important to you. It will keep your life goals front-of-mind versus nowhere to be seen, and the measurement will serve as either a confidence builder or an awareness creator—both great for your brand.

Plan to plan a planning day today.

73. To avoid putting unnecessary black marks on your brand, leave a little room for error. In fact, leave as much room as you can get.

One of the more common breakdowns having a big effect on our success is not delivering a project on time or delivering a simply acceptable level of quality as specified and expected. In some cases it's difficult, even impossible, to recover from this kind of debacle, depending on what was at stake and who was affected. Generally at the end of any broken agreement or poor performance, there are not only people who you are directly working with who were affected, but others who you don't see, and those can be the ones who bring you to a write-up or worse.

> A commitment without built-in room for error will more often end up as a broken commitment.

There are two parts of every project delivery. First is the amount of time we commit to have something happen, and second is the time we give those on the project team to accomplish what is needed, part and parcel, for the "total delivery promise." Having delivered thousands of projects, I've learned that it's best to exercise that old but still-relevant principle: under-commit and over-deliver. When someone gives me a project and requests a lead time, I rarely give an immediate answer because that isn't what they are looking for. What they need is a *definitive answer*—one that they can absolutely count on. Once they know your commitment was well thought out instead of improvised, they'll be more inclined to trust it.

There's a bit of psychology here, but the science is that people will spontaneously give you time frames that are not what they really need, nor might they give you the time to get the project done right. As the doer, it's imperative, when possible, to control the time frame and always give yourself a 15–25 percent buffer in case there's a problem in the process. This not only improves your chances of getting it done right, it also gives you the opportunity to improve your brand by over-delivering. Of course, by doing a little inquiry you can usually find out the actual timeline. In some cases it may be a legitimate rush, but more often, it is not. Those you work with will value the consistency in your delivery over the speed, and if they had to choose, consistency would win consistently.

> Every time we break a commitment, we
> put a crack in our character.

Once you create some wiggle room with the stakeholder, there's the issue of delegating timelines with those on team-based projects tasked to ensure the delivery happens well. In my world, I work with dozens of internal and external personnel—all that in some way hold the keys to drive my brand right into the limelight or straight into the ground. It all depends on whether they deliver excellence on their part of the process. That's the only way I can deliver on mine. Some projects I work on can have a dozen delegations, so there are lots of moving parts and lots of room for error. The key here (and it may seem hypocritical given the previous paragraph) is to let all players on the deliverables team know that you need the project 15–25 percent in advance of the actual timeline. Always create an adequate buffer. In fact, it's wise to build in enough time that if someone gets hit by a train (God forbid) you'd be left with enough time to get a replacement. This way you can delegate to a new resource and get that part of the project handled so those you work with remain in good standing while keeping your brand shining, not fading.

It also helps to specify and calendar the actual items to be produced to ensure everyone's on schedule and is delivering what is needed. You can develop a shortcut signature in your email program that says something like,

Hey <name>, just wanted to make sure the <project> you're working on is on schedule for <time frame>. If you have any issues with that or need any help, please contact me immediately. And also, please let me know you received this email. Thanks again for your excellence on the project.

It may seem like a bit of extra trouble, but it pales in comparison to the trouble created when a project or initiative under your watch underperforms in any way.

 Create a little more room for error to fortify your commitments today.

74. Consider that your brand at work has a tone— one that is worth listening to, or not.

Ever meet someone for the first time, but before you meet, you remember that you heard good things about them? At this point, without even knowing them personally, they've installed a positive tone of anticipation based on what you've heard. After you met and had a pleasant exchange you noticed the words you heard about them aligned with the person you met. Truthfully, you didn't have any real background on them. In fact, for all you knew they could have been a con artist or a Mother Teresa type, yet the tone remained pleasant. The next time you saw them they dressed nicely again, greeted you authentically, and asked if they could help in any way. In an instant, the tone improved and the sound got better. In fact, you noticed it would be nice to be around that tone, share the tone with others, and help that tone in any way you could.

> Small things add up to a big difference like little dietary decisions help add to a longer life.

We all resonate with others in a tone. In fact, in this realm no one is tone-deaf. Everyone around us gives off a tone we either want more of, don't care much for, or react against. Take, let's say, Bob, for example—a guy whose profanity always seems to come out at the wrong time. He gossips about others and disguises it in a form of corporate protection, saying, "Watch out for this person or that person." He dresses okay, makes excuses for his poor work performance, and generally when he approaches a group or walks into a room he brings a tone that's off-key; people do their best to shut off the noise, and in some cases they'll do what it takes to turn the noise off for good.

Having been in branding my whole life, this accurately describes the level of detail associated with building your brand at work. The demise of a brand is rarely one big event. For instance, let's look at Tylenol. In the early '80s, six adults and one child died as a result of taking Tylenol. Talk about a horrific tone playing over the brand in the media around the world. The tragedy (beyond the obvious) was that Tylenol was not at fault. It was due to someone (who was never caught) poisoning the bottles with potassium cyanide. However, when you have an event of that magnitude associated with your brand, the kind of tone that plays across the airwaves of the world can take you out of the game in an instant.

Impressively, and with great care and responsibility, Tylenol went on the offensive and started casting a new tone that revolutionized an industry. They added safety mechanisms to their packaging that would ensure consumers would know if the package had been tampered with. They didn't just create a safer product, they birthed a safety movement emulated by many. Despite the naysayers broadcasting that Tylenol was, in essence, *toast*, their product today remains among the top pain relievers in the country, and their market share remains where it was before the crisis, as it should be. They delivered in an exemplary manner. Today, there's no negative tone associated with Tylenol. And yet, had they played poorly with the wrong note, they may never have been heard from again.

> Play to a positive new tune at work today. In fact, put "notes" everywhere to remind yourself.

Currently, you have a tone at work. It's based on all the aspects we've covered so far and more. Some people have a tone in the office that resembles a beautiful tune, while others resemble that of nails on a chalkboard. Again, the saving grace here is that it's rarely a single large event that can bring a tone to a screeching sound, but more a composition of bad play and off notes in a diversity of circumstances that clues people in that more bad notes are coming. Regardless of where you are on the scale, you can start creating a tone that resonates and illuminates rather than exacerbates and alienates so those around can tune in rather than tune out.

Play a new and improved tune at work today.

75. Deciding who you will be and how you will contribute to a meeting in advance is the beginning of a *brilliant* meeting.

If I had a dollar for every time I stumbled into a meeting without much clarity on the meeting agenda or my contribution to the meeting, I'd be ashamed at how much I had . . . many hundreds of dollars at a minimum. Meetings are those things we either casually enter into, or we steward over them with clear purpose and care. If you think about the foundation of our work and what moves it, meetings are the driving force of just about everything that happens. But how we manage them before, during, and after is where we waste time, money, and opportunity—which prompts books called *Death by Meeting* and other slams on this most important driver of business progress. So what makes a meeting successful?

1. A meeting is successful by nature of the right parties being invited to the room. Anyone not contributing at the level of excellence expected in the meeting is a liability to the room and will polarize progress and impede rhythm.

2. A meeting needs a clear agenda of what will take place in the meeting, the actual goal or outcome desired from the meeting, and (as we've covered) who is expected to contribute what and when during the time—all delivered well in advance so people have time to prepare and bring their full value to the process. The agenda is critical: the more specific the agenda, the more seriously those in attendance will take it.

3. It's important to make sure there is written and cc'ed account-ability for who is going to do what based on the tasks defined in the meeting, along with timelines and details that will produce best results.

4. A helpful, but not necessary, step is a follow-up with the total group sharing gratitude for their contribution in the meeting as well as the results that came from the gathering. This way, the next meeting that is called with this team will have nothing left undone, all loops closed, and everyone feeling good about "killing it" once again. This is what I call "Life by Meeting."

> Meetings called without serious attention to detail
> will always fail in meeting expectations.

The biggest factor of meeting success, in addition to the specifics we covered, is to be clear about your way of being in any meeting. For example, several years ago my business partners and I entered into a venture-capital deal to start a financial services company. It was our first rodeo. On our second pitch the investor pulled out his checkbook and wrote a check for $1 million. After six months, we learned that the investor brought to the table (through a reputable investment firm) was involved in an illegal business which none of us—including the investment firm—knew about.

After the shock to our system wore off, I said to my partners, "We need to get out of this company and fast." However, my partners (rightfully so) wanted to either maintain interest in the company or somehow get bought out of the deal. I agreed I'd like to get something, but I was pretty resolute it would be best if we could negotiate an immediate hold-harmless agreement and be off the corporate documents sooner than later. I also told them I felt it best that we went into the interim board meeting with a disposition of listening and accommodation and not one of contention. The result? We ended the meeting in clear, unstrained agreement, and a week later we were out of the deal completely and legally.

Several months later I got a call from one of the parties telling me that they were all fired by six guys who came into their tenth-floor office with exposed (permitted) weapons for intimidation. The company was gutted and our ex-partners were ultimately saddled with several hundred thousand dollars of financial liabilities. There were even death threats flying around, and yet we were long gone, didn't have a shred of liability or attachment to the group, didn't even get a call—all because we knew the agenda, had the right parties in the room, decided on our way of being, were clear about the desired outcome, and nailed down detailed next steps.

Ultimately, it was the preparing of our hearts, minds, and strategies for the meeting that made it a quick exit without any real issues. We were very intentional about what we wanted to have happen by when, which is why it was received well on the other end.

There is compound value in deciding in advance the way we will act and the things we will say (and often more importantly, *not* say), as well as imagining the meeting in our minds as a sort of dress rehearsal. The value in practice is that we can identify what may happen, what things may be said, what curveballs may be thrown, and be ready for them in such a way that our meeting performance will have us invited into more important meetings. After all, if meetings are the driving force of business, it stands to reason that our desire is to find ourselves in more important meetings where the upside of our involvement means more of everything we want.

 Think through your meetings and bring a focused intentionality to them today.

76. Don't be a conversation hijacker—it'll never fly.

Conversation skills are *not* something we typically believe we can improve instantly. The reason is obvious. Everyone we talk to is different. Their moods, emotions, circumstances, and life realities change from conversation to conversation, making communication challenging and totally unpredictable. But I believe we can improve our skills instantly if we eliminate a common and destructive practice in listening that you'll probably experience before the day is done.

> Conversations that aren't a two-way street often end up on a one-way dead-end street.

Ever been in a conversation with someone only to have the person you're talking to change the direction of the conversation toward them every time there's a change in topic? You're trying to create two-way relatability, and there doesn't seem to be any interest for them to remain in your world for a while and go deeper into the topic you're sharing about or get further into your life. There's an odd recoil in which everything said, whether you bring it up or not, ends up in their world, their experiences, and their point of view.

I call this Conversational Hijacking (C-Jacking). It's no fun to be in a conversation with someone who perpetrates this self-centered behavior that rips the reward out of conversational potential. So what's it look like, this *C-Jacking*? Let's say I'm talking with someone and the conversation is leading in the direction of problems with bosses. I share that I had a problem with my boss last week. A C-Jacker wouldn't inquire how I was doing with that, ask more questions to get further context so they could help, or show any signs of caring. In fact, they would bounce right into an experience they had that was similar or nod and say something patronizing like, "Yeah, I get it," before changing to a different topic they'd like to discuss.

One time I met someone at a party and they began to C-Jack the conversation. It was going to be a long night, so as an experiment, I wanted to see how often they would C-Jack my topic. It happened six times in various forms, and the conversation lasted for about twenty minutes. Given this was an experiment, I wasn't annoyed as much as I was fascinated by how disconnected a human being could be and how little interest they could show in someone else. The ratio was about 5/95: I spoke about 5 percent of the time, and they dragged everything I mentioned into their world for the remaining 95 percent. I enjoyed the experience a lot, especially when it was over.

> Until we push the limits of caring in conversation, we'll never know the value of what may exist there.

Now I consider myself a pretty adequate conversationalist, but thought to myself, do I do that? The answer came back quickly that I do on occasion. It's not chronic, but sometimes out of self-centeredness or nervousness, I notice that instead of staying in their world for a while and exploring the possibility of what is there, I shift the topic in my direction without staying very close to what they are talking about. I notice when this happens, the other seems to shut down and resign themselves to the idea of tolerating the conversation rather than engaging in it.

There is a more genuine option available, and that is for me to forget about what I want to leverage from a conversation and make the only agenda I have *their agenda*. One thing is certain: when I'm tempted to C-Jack conversations I immediately notice a presence of stress and generally leave these word battles feeling unfulfilled, as I'm sure they do. But when I stay on their topic, expand on it a bit and explore it with them, conversations don't unnerve me; in fact, I feel excited because I get to bring the undistracted me to reside for a time in somebody else's world. It's a peaceful place. I get to forget about my crazy world for a while, and these conversations usually end in a perfect balance of mutual exchange and value.

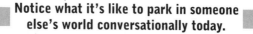 **Notice what it's like to park in someone else's world conversationally today.**

77. We don't suddenly find ourselves in trouble. Decision by decision, we choose ourselves into trouble, then suddenly realize it.*

These days, it appears blaming others and things outside ourselves for the challenging situations we "find ourselves in" is on the rise. People who don't want to account for the results in their lives are going to great lengths and getting pretty creative with how they spin their current situation. "It's the government's fault." "Corporate America is evil." "The country is to blame." "My boss was the problem." "Clients should be more loyal." "Liberals are the cause." "Conservatives are making the rich richer and me poorer." And so it goes.

Unfortunately, no matter how good the spin, blame, or attribution may sound, there is zero hope in placing responsibility anywhere outside of ourselves for what happens to us. In contrast, there is an abundance of promise in building a strong resilience into life by accounting for everything under our watch. It's not something we have to do (as free will is real), but it is something we get to do, and the upside will lead to a career and life that have more freedom, control, and actual progress instead of being highly skilled in the blame game.

> It is our upbringing and experiences that give us our point of view. It is the decisions we make daily that comprise the brand we are and the success we have.

*Note: In this point I am not referring to victims of abuse, crime, illness, or things beyond people's control.

Several years back a few friends of mine, Dan Tocchini, Derek Watson, and Larry Pinci, self-published a book called *Killing the Victim before the Victim Kills You.*

The premise of the book is that entertaining a victim stance regarding where you are in life will kill the possibility in you and around you. It removes the potential to become more effective at navigating and driving your life because you've turned the accelerator, brakes, and wheels over to others . . . *many who can't drive.*

This is the state of countless victims today who, for example, are counting on government to be their provider when the only governmental solution that is durable and predictable is "self-government": governing our own behaviors to have the life we want to have despite what happens in the circus arena of politics. We are victim to nothing except how we think and relate to things. There are times we may hold ourselves hostage to limitations because in the moment it seems easier to blame someone or something rather than to own up to our performance and results. But owning our performance is the place where hope lives.

I once worked with an individual who was leading a team on a big project. The due date was approaching, so he called a meeting to check the progress of the team. Five of the team members were on task; two weren't, and one of the two was nowhere near where they needed to be. Between the two breakdowns, the project had to be postponed and the client notified. A lot of people weren't happy, including the team leader. This was a big hit on his internal and external brand, and he repeatedly made it known that he was not at fault for the delay but was a victim of a couple of players who failed to do their job.

In sitting down and going over his process, I requested two pieces of information: First, was the project schedule in writing with dates and timelines? Next, was there written documentation outlining the specific nature of what was going to be done by whom and when? He quickly responded that he hadn't updated the project schedule because he had been so busy, and the project descriptions were given verbally in the kickoff meeting. When I asked him what his checkpoints were along the way to ensure the job was on track, there was no clear process for that either. Turns out he was a victim of his own inefficiency, and the learning lesson should prohibit that in the future. He should quickly get rid of the victim mentality before the victim mentality gets rid of him.

> The "new me" is always a decision away.

We all understand the principle that we reap what we sow. It's pretty critical that in any breakdown we're a part of, we need to look closely at the way we participated in it. There are times where we are flat-out at fault and other times where we are a small percentage of the problem: either we caused it, allowed it, or our complacency made room for the problem to occur. It's senseless and shows a lack of humility when we try to avoid taking responsibility for what our part is, regardless of the percentage of involvement. We learn a great deal more when we are willing to readily own up to our part in things. Through this discipline, no matter what is going on and how bad it is, we will always be in a position of control, strength, and truth.

Consider self-government as your biggest opportunity today.

The final word . . .

Of all the differences we can make with others, the best one is always the next one.

If you've made it to this page, chances are you've received enough value from this book to consider sharing it with someone else. There are a few ways to do that. One is to photocopy or scan a page, or snap a shot of a point and send it to someone who it might resonate with. I'm sure as you were reading, you thought to yourself, *Hmm, this point reminds me of so and so,* or *This is so them.* It's always a risk to share something that intends to bring a new perspective or improvement, but great brands don't play just to play, they play to win in life, and risk is part of the successful person's daily process. The truth is, the world needs more people who are willing to risk sharing insights that matter, regardless of who writes or says them.

> Never underestimate the value of giving someone
> a brief, relevant point to improve their life.

Another way is to give the copy you've read away to someone. The bigger we give, the bigger our peace, joy, and every other great thing we'd like to have more of. Yet a third option is to buy a copy for someone (or at least tell others about it and write a good review so others are inclined to buy it).

Regardless of whether you do any of these things, I'm grateful you've read my book, and if you decide to pay it forward, I would appreciate that. My vision has never been to be in the bookselling business per se; it has always been to make more of a positive difference with others. Within *that vision* is my ask.

A word on the brand of me and some of my business brands.

My brother Dave (the CPA) got the left-brain gene in the family. As for the brand of me, I'm a right-brain creative thinker, meaning I lean more lunar than linear, more pictures than spreadsheets, less logical and more philosophical. I started in business as a graphic designer, then turned writer, turned creative director, and turned large ad agency cofounder and CEO—picking up a few of those "left-brain" skills along the way. It's positioned me as a pragmatic marketing strategist and brand creator who's developed hundreds of brands and has been responsible for marketing budgets from ten thousand a month to a million a month and everything in between. *What a ride, and I'm still on it.*

Today, I run a boutique branding agency (breviti.com) that does all things branding and assists with marketing and revenue-generation strategy or implementation. I am also an equity partner in a world-class live-action and motion-graphics video agency (veracitycolab .com) that does breakthrough video work for clients around the world and was recently voted number 1 video agency in the country.

My journey as an author started with "personal development" emails sent to a moderately sized audience of clients, vendors, and whoever would read it. While talking with an author friend who'd been reading them and who wanted to try his hand as a literary agent, we agreed I'd be his first client. Long story short, we submitted a book proposal for *Shift Your Thinking*, and eighteen months later, I was an author.

Like any good agent, Joey told me, "Anyone can be a one-time author—everyone has **one** book in them—but are you a writer?" Thus, *Shift Your Thinking for Success* is here, and the next *Shift Your Thinking*–themed book (which releases in Summer 2019)—a book of biblically based principles to better all aspects of our time on the planet—will be out soon.

The "why" behind me finds few things more rewarding than helping people get from Point (A)nywhere to Point (B)etter in life, business, and relationships. With the audacity of having the personal mission statement that reads, "To be a graceful interruption to whatever's not working in someone's business or personal life," I'm committed to stopping the trajectory of anyone headed for difficulty and helping turn them toward the path of least resistance and most profitability in life and relationships. I'll talk to anyone, anytime, about anything, knowing something good will come from an authentic conversation.

I still write those emails, but now they're mostly just one-liner quotes designed to provoke change and reengineer thinking. If you'd like to get those emails, visit deandelsesto.com/contact and sign up.

As for speaking engagements, I'll speak to small groups and large audiences. If you believe my brand of thinking might resonate in your sphere of influence, feel free to reach out. My main talks focus on personal branding, business branding, leadership, and business performance and are anywhere from twenty to ninety minutes for audiences of any size. I also offer smaller group sessions at companies and organizations training leaders and executive teams from one to three and a half hours. You can learn more at my personal website (deandelsesto.com).

That's it for now. I wish you the best on your journey of life, and thank you again for reading *Shift Your Thinking for Success*.

Dean

Dean Del Sesto has been in marketing, branding, and corporate development for his entire career. Today, he runs an award-winning branding agency called Breviti (www.breviti.com) and is also a partner in VeracityColab, a B2B and consumer based video agency (www.veracitycolab.com). With over 25 years in the field, Dean has had the pleasure to be directly involved in the local to enterprise-wide brand development of over 800 companies and still loves it today.

Dean has a passion for business advisory board involvement and speaks nationally on a variety of topics including personal and business branding, marketing, leadership, and improving relationships. He and his wife have been married almost 25 years and live in Orange County, California.

SMALL CHANGES,
BIG IMPACT

We all want to grow, improve, and succeed, yet so often the things we tell ourselves seem to stop our dreams in their tracks. But that can change. These 200 to-the-point readings will help you shift your thoughts and behaviors so you can change the course of your life, work, and relationships—for good.

Learn more at **DEANDELSESTO.COM**

DEAN DEL SESTO ™

SHIFT INTO OVERTHRIVE™